W9-CFL-407

MORE HIGH SCHOOL

TALKSHEETS

—Updated!

50
CREATIVE DISCUSSIONS FOR
HIGH SCHOOL YOUTH GROUPS

DAVID LYNN

ZondervanPublishing House
Grand Rapids, Michigan

A Division of HarperCollins*Publishers*

More High School TalkSheets—Updated! 50 creative discussions for junior high youth groups

Copyright © 2001 by Youth Specialties

Youth Specialties books, 300 S. Pierce St., El Cajon, CA 92020, are published by Zondervan Publishing House, 5300 Patterson Ave. S.E., Grand Rapids, MI 49530.

Library of Congress Cataloging-in-Publication Data

Lynn, David, 1954-
    More high school talksheets—updated! : 50 creative discussion starters for youth groups
/ David Lynn.
      p. cm.
    ISBN 0-310-23854-4
    1. Church work with teenagers. 2. High school students—Religious life. I. Title.

BV4447 .L9635 2001
268'.433—dc21

00-043939

All Scripture quotations, unless otherwise noted, are taken from the *Holy Bible: New International Version* (North American Edition). Copyright © 1973, 1978, 1984 by the International Bible Society. Used by permission of Zondervan Bible Publishers.

The TalkSheets appearing in this book may be photocopied for local use in churches, youth groups, and other Christian education activities. Special permission for reproduction is not necessary. However, no part of this publication may be reproduced, stored in a retrieval system, or transmitted in any form or by any means—electronic, mechanical, photocopy, recording, or any other—except for brief quotations in printed reviews, without the prior permission of the publisher. All rights reserved.

Web site addresses listed in this book were current at the time of publication, but we can't guarantee they're still operational. If you have trouble with an URL, please contact us via e-mail (YS@YouthSpecialties.com) to let us know if you've found the current or new URL or if the URL is no longer operational.

Edited by Mary Fletcher, Anita Palmer, and Tamara Rice
Interior and cover design by PAZ Design Group
Illustrations and borders by Rick Sealock

Printed in the United States of America

03 04 05 06 07 /VG/ 10 9 8 7 6 5

CONTENTS

MORE HIGH SCHOOL TALKSHEETS —Updated!

THE HOWS AND WHATS OF TALKSHEETS

You are holding a very valuable book! No, it won't make you a genius or millionaire. But it does contain 50 instant discussions for junior high and middle school kids. Inside you'll find reproducible TalkSheets that cover a variety of hot topics—plus simple, step-by-step instructions on how to use them. All you need is this book, a few copies of the handouts, and some kids (and maybe a snack or two). You're on your way to landing on some serious issues in kids' lives today.

These TalkSheets are user-friendly and very flexible. They can be used in a youth group meeting, a Sunday school class, or in a Bible study group. You can adapt them for either large or small groups. And, they can be fully covered in only 20 minutes or more intensively in two hours.

You can build an entire youth group meeting around a single TalkSheet, or you can use TalkSheets to supplement other materials and resources you might be using. These are tools for you—how you use them is your choice.

More High School TalkSheets—Updated! is not your average curriculum or workbook. This collection of discussions will get your kids involved and excited about talking through important issues. The TalkSheets deal with key topics and include interesting activities, challenging questions, and eye-catching graphics. They will challenge your kids to think about opinions, learn about themselves, and grow in their faith.

LEADING A TALKSHEET DISCUSSION

TalkSheets can be used as a curriculum for your youth group, but they are designed to be springboards for discussion. They encourage your kids to take part and interact with each other while talking about real life issues. And hopefully they'll do some serious thinking, discover new ideas for themselves, defend their points of view, and make decisions.

Youth today face a world of moral confusion. Youth leaders must teach the church's beliefs and values—and also help young people make the right choices in a world with so many options. Teenagers are bombarded with the voices of society and media messages—most of which drown out what they hear from the church.

A TalkSheet discussion works for this very reason. While dealing with the questions and activities on the TalkSheet, your kids will think carefully about issues, compare their beliefs and values with others, and make their own choices. TalkSheets will challenge your group to explain and rework their ideas in a Christian atmosphere of acceptance, support, and growth.

The most common fear of junior high and middle school youth group leaders is, "What will I do if the kids in my group just sit there and don't say anything?" Well, when kids don't have anything to say, it's because they haven't had a chance to get their thoughts organized! Most young people haven't developed the ability to think on their feet. Since many are afraid they might sound stupid, they don't know how to voice their ideas and opinions.

The solution? TalkSheets let your kids deal with the issues in a challenging, non-threatening way before the actual discussion begins. They'll have time to organize their thoughts, write them down, and ease their fears about participating. They may even look forward to sharing their answers! Most importantly, they'll (most likely) want to find out what others said and open up to talk through the topics.

If you're still a little leery about the success of a real discussion among your kids, that's okay! The only way to get them rolling is to get them started.

YOUR ROLE AS THE LEADER

The best discussions don't happen by accident. They require careful preparation and a sensitive leader. Don't worry if you aren't experienced or don't have hours to prepare.

TalkSheets are designed to help even the novice leader! The more TalkSheet discussions you lead, the easier it becomes. Keep the following tips in mind when using the TalkSheets as you get your kids talking.

BE CHOOSY

Each TalkSheet deals with a different topic. Choose a TalkSheet based on the needs and the maturity level of your group. Don't feel obligated to use the TalkSheets in the order they appear in this book. Use your best judgment and mix them up however you want—they are tools for you!

TRY IT YOURSELF

Once you have chosen a TalkSheet for your group, answer the questions and do the activities yourself. Imagine your kids' reactions to the TalkSheet. This will help you prepare for the discussion and understand what you are asking them to do. Plus, you'll have some time to think of other appropriate questions, activities, and Bible verses.

GET SOME INSIGHT

On each leader's guide page, you'll find numerous tips and ideas for getting the most out of your discussion. You may want to add some of your own thoughts or ideas in the margins. And, there's room to keep track of the date and the name of your group at the top of the leader's page. You'll also find suggestions for additional activities and discussion questions.

There are some references to Internet links throughout the TalkSheets. These are guides for you to find the resources and information that you need. For additional help, be sure to visit the Youth Specialties Web site at www.YouthSpecialties.com for information on materials and further links to finding what you need.

MAKE COPIES

Kids will need their own copy of the TalkSheet. Only make copies of the student's side of the TalkSheet! The material on the reverse side (the leader's guide) is just for you. You're able to make copies for your group because we've given you permission to do so. U.S. copyright laws have not changed, and it is still mandatory to request permission from a publisher before making copies of other published material. It is against the law not to do so. However, permission is given for you to make copies of this material for your group only, not for every youth group in your state. Thank you for cooperating.

INTRODUCE THE TOPIC

It's important to introduce the topic before you pass out the TalkSheets to your group. Depending on your group, keep it short and to the point. Be careful not to over-introduce the topic, sound preachy, or resolve the issue before you've started. Your goal is to spark their interest and leave plenty of room for discussion.

The best way to do this is verbally. You can tell a story, share an experience, or describe a situation or problem having to do with the topic. You might want to jump-start your group by asking something like, "What is the first thing you think of when you hear the word _____ [insert the topic]?" Then, after a few answers have been given, you can add something like, "Well, it seems we all have different ideas about this subject. Tonight we're going to investigate it a bit further..." Then pass out the TalkSheet and be sure that everyone has a pencil or pen. Now you're on your way! The following are excellent methods you can use to introduce any topic in this book—

- Show a related short film or video.
- Read a passage from a book or magazine that relates to the subject.
- Play a popular CD that deals with the topic.
- Perform a short skit or dramatic presentation.
- Play a simulation game or role-play, setting up the topic.
- Present current statistics, survey results, or read a current newspaper article that provides recent information about the topic.
- Use a crowd-breaker or game, getting into the topic in a humorous way. For example if the topic is fun, play a game to begin the discussion. If the topic is success, consider a

game that helps the kids experience success or failure.

- Use posters, videos, or any other visuals to help focus attention on the topic.

There are endless possibilities for an intro—you are limited only by your own creativity! Each TalkSheet offers a few suggestions, but you are free to use any method with which you feel most comfortable. But do keep in mind that the introduction is a very important part of each session.

SET BOUNDARIES

It'll be helpful to set a few ground rules before the discussion. Keep the rules to a minimum, of course, but let the kids know what's expected of them. Here are suggestions for some basic ground rules—

- **What is said in this room stays in this room.** Emphasize the importance of confidentiality. Some kids will open up, some won't. Confidentiality is vital for a good discussion. If your kids can't keep the discussion in the room, then they won't open up.
- **No put-downs.** Mutual respect is important. If your kids disagree with some opinions, ask them to comment on the subject (but not on the other person). It's okay to oppose the ideas, but not to attack other people.
- **There is no such thing as a dumb question.** Your group members must feel free to ask questions at any time. The best way to learn is to ask questions and get answers.
- **No one is forced to talk.** Let everyone know they have the right to pass or not answer any question.
- **Only one person speaks at a time.** This is a mutual respect issue. Everyone's opinion is worthwhile and deserves to be heard.

Communicate with your group that everyone needs to respect these boundaries. If you sense that your group members are attacking each other or getting a negative attitude during the discussion, do stop and deal with the problem before going on.

ALLOW ENOUGH TIME

Pass out copies of the TalkSheet to your kids after the introduction and make sure that each person has a pen or pencil and a Bible. There are usually five or six activities on each TalkSheet. If your time

is limited, or if you are using only a part of the TalkSheet, tell the group to complete only the activities you'd like them to.

Decide ahead of time whether or not you would like the kids to work on the TalkSheets individually or in groups.

Let them know how much time they have for completing the TalkSheet and let them know when there is a minute (or so) left. Go ahead and give them some extra time and then start the discussion when everyone seems ready to go.

SET THE STAGE

Create a climate of acceptance. Most teenagers are afraid to voice their opinions because they don't want to be laughed at or look stupid in front of their peers. They want to feel safe if they're going to share their feelings and beliefs. Communicate that they can share their thoughts and ideas—even if they may be different or unpopular. If your kids get put-downs, criticism, laughter, or snide comments (even if their statements are opposed to the teachings of the Bible) it'll hurt the discussion.

Always phrase your questions—even those that are printed on the TalkSheets—so that you are asking for an opinion, not an answer. For example if a question reads, "What should Bill have done in that situation?" change it to, "What do you think Bill should have done in that situation?" The simple addition of the three words "do you think" makes the question less threatening and a matter of opinion, rather than a demand for the right answer. Your kids will relax when they will feel more comfortable and confident. Plus, they'll know that you actually care about their opinions and they'll feel appreciated!

LEAD THE DISCUSSION

Discuss the TalkSheet with the group and encourage all your kids to participate. Communicate that it's important for them to respect each other's opinions and feelings! The more they contribute, the better the discussion will be.

If your youth group is big, you may divide it into smaller groups of six to 12. Each of these small groups should have a facilitator—either an adult leader or a student member—to keep the discussion going. Remind the facilitators not to dominate the others. If the group looks to the facilitator for an answer, ask him or her to direct the questions or responses back to the group. Once the smaller groups have completed their discussions, combine them into one large group and ask the different groups to share their ideas.

You don't have to divide the groups up with every TalkSheet. For some discussions, you may want to vary the group size and or divide the meeting into groups of the same sex.

The discussion should target the questions and answers on the TalkSheet. Go through them one at a time and ask the kids to share their responses. Have them compare their answers and brainstorm new ones in addition to the ones they've written down. Encourage them to share their opinions and answers, but don't force those who are quiet.

AFFIRM ALL RESPONSES—RIGHT OR WRONG

Let your kids know that their comments and contributions are appreciated and important. This is especially true for those who rarely speak up in group activities. Make a point of thanking them for joining in. This will be an incentive for them to participate further.

Remember that affirmation doesn't mean approval. Affirm even those comments that seem wrong to you. You'll show that everyone has a right to express their ideas—no matter how controversial they may be. If someone states an opinion that is off base, make a mental note of the comment. Then in your wrap-up, come back to the comment or present a different point of view in a positive way. But don't reprimand the student who voiced the comment.

DON'T BE THE AUTHORITATIVE ANSWER

Some kids think you have the right answer to every question. They'll look to you for approval, even when they are answering another group member's question. If they start to focus on you for answers, redirect them toward the group by making a comment like, "Remember that you're talking to everyone, not just me."

Your goal as the facilitator is to keep the discussion alive and kicking. It's important that your kids think of you as a member of the group—on their level. The less authoritative you are, the

more value your own opinions will have. If your kids view you as a peer, they will listen to your comments. You have a tremendous responsibility to be, with sincerity, their trusted friend.

LISTEN TO EACH PERSON

God gave you one mouth and two ears. Good discussion leaders know how to listen. Although it's tempting at times, don't monopolize the discussion. Encourage others to talk first—then express your opinions during your wrap up.

DON'T FORCE IT

Encourage all your kids to talk, but don't make them comment. Each member has the right to pass. If you feel that the discussion isn't going well, go on to the next question or restate the question to keep them moving.

DON'T TAKE SIDES

You'll probably have different opinions expressed in the group from time to time. Be extra careful not to take one side or another. Encourage both sides to think through their positions—ask questions to get them deeper. If everyone agrees on an issue, you can play devil's advocate with tough questions and stretch their thinking. Remain neutral—your point of view is your own, not that of the group.

DON'T LET ANYONE (INCLUDING YOU) TAKE OVER

Nearly every youth group has one person who likes to talk and is perfectly willing to express an opinion on any subject. Try to encourage equal participation from all the kids.

SET UP FOR THE TALK

Make sure that the seating arrangement is inclusive and encourages a comfortable, safe atmosphere for discussion. Theater-style seating (in rows) isn't discussion-friendly. Instead, arrange the chairs in a circle or semicircle (or on the floor with pillows!).

LET THEM LAUGH!

Discussions can be fun! Most of the TalkSheets include questions that'll make them laugh and get them thinking, too.

LET THEM BE SILENT

Silence can be a scary for discussion leaders! Some react by trying to fill the silence with a question or a comment. The following suggestions may help you to handle silence more effectively—

- Be comfortable with silence. Wait it out for 30 seconds or so to respond. You may want to restate the question to give your kids a gentle nudge.
- Talk about the silence with the group. What does the silence mean? Do they really not have any comments? Maybe they're confused, embarrassed, or don't want to share.
- Answer the silence with questions or comments like, "I know this is challenging to think about..." or "It's scary to be the first to talk." If you acknowledge the silence, it may break the ice.
- Ask a different question that may be easier to handle or that will clarify the one already posed. But don't do this too quickly without giving them time to think the first one through.

KEEP IT UNDER CONTROL

Monitor the discussion. Be aware if the discussion is going in a certain direction or off track. This can happen fast, especially if the kids disagree or things get heated. Mediate wisely and set the tone that you want. If your group gets bored with an issue, get them back on track. Let the discussion unfold, but be sensitive to your group and who is or is not getting involved.

If a student brings up a side issue that's interesting, decide whether or not to purse it. If discussion is going well and the issue is worth discussion, let them talk it through. But, if things get way off track, say something like, "Let's come back to that subject later if we have time. Right now, let's finish our discussion on..."

BE CREATIVE AND FLEXIBLE

You don't have to follow the order of the questions on the TalkSheet. Follow your own creative instinct. If you find other ways to use the TalkSheets, use them! Go ahead and add other questions or Bible references.

Don't feel pressured to spend time on every single activity. If you're short on time, you can skip some items. Stick with the questions that are the most interesting to the group.

SET YOUR GOALS

TalkSheets are designed to move along toward a goal, but you need to identify your goal in advance. What would you like your young people to learn? What truth should they discover? What is the goal of the session? If you don't know where you're going, it's doubtful you will get there.

BE THERE FOR YOUR KIDS

Some kids may want to talk more with you (you got 'em thinking!). Let them know that you can talk one-on-one with them afterwards.

Communicate to the kids that they can feel free to talk with you about anything with confidentiality. Let them know you're there for them with support and concern, even after the TalkSheet discussion has been completed.

USE THE BIBLE

Most adults believe the Bible has authority over their lives. It's common for adults to start their discussions or to support their arguments with Bible verses. But today's teenagers form their opinions and beliefs from their own life situations first—then they decide how the Bible fits their needs. TalkSheets start with the realities of the adolescent world and then move toward the Bible. You'll be able to show them that the Bible can be their guide and that God does have something to say to them about their own unique situations.

The last activity on each TalkSheet uses Bible verses that were chosen for their application to each issue. But they aren't exhaustive. Feel free to add whatever other verses you think would fit well and add to the discussion.

After your kids read the verses, ask them to think how the verses apply to their lives and summarize the meanings for them.
For example, after reading the passage for "Livin' It Up," you may summarize by saying something like, "See? God wants us to have fun! In fact, Jesus spoke in his parables of feasts, dancing, and celebration. It's obvious that God wants Christians to have good times—but to be careful, too."

CLOSE THE DISCUSSION

Present a challenge to the group by asking yourself, "What do I want the kids to remember most from this discussion?" There's your wrap-up! It's important to conclude by affirming the group and offering a summary that ties the discussion together.

Sometimes you won't need a wrap-up. You may want to leave the issue hanging and discuss it in another meeting. That way, your group can think about it more and you can nail down the final ideas later.

TAKE IT FURTHER

On the leader's guide page, you'll find additional discussion activities—labeled More—for following up on the discussion. These aren't a must, but highly recommended. They let the kids reflect upon, evaluate, review, and assimilate what they've learned. These activities may lead to more discussion and better learning.

After you've done the activity, be sure to debrief your kids on the activity, either now or at the next group meeting. A few good questions to ask about the activity are—

- What happened when you did this activity or discussion?

- Was it helpful or a waste of time?

- How did you feel when doing the activity or discussion?

- Did the activity/discussion make you think differently or affect you in any way?

- In one sentence state what you learned from this activity or discussion.

A FINAL WORD TO THE WISE — THAT'S YOU!

Some of these TalkSheets deal with topics that may be sensitive or controversial for your kids. Issues like sexuality or materialism aren't discussed openly in some churches. You're encouraging discussion and inviting your kids to express their opinions. As a result, you may be criticized by parents or others in your church who may not see the importance of such discussions. Use your best judgment. If you suspect that a particular TalkSheet will cause problems, you may not want to use it. Or you may want to tweak a particular TalkSheet and only cover some of the questions. Either way, the potential bad could outweigh the good—better safe than sorry. To avoid any misunderstanding, you may want to give the parents or senior pastor (or whoever else you are accountable to) copies of the TalkSheet before you use it. Let them know the discussion you would like to have and the goal you are hoping to accomplish. Challenge your kids to take their TalkSheet home to talk about it with their parents. How would their parents, as young people, have answered the questions? Your kids may find that their parents understand them better than they thought! Also, encourage them to think of other Bible verses or ways that the TalkSheet applies to their lives.

BREAKIN' THE RULES

1. What do you do to feel **rebellious**?
   - ❑ Listen to loud music
   - ❑ Surf the Internet—and go where I want
   - ❑ Watch an R or NC-17 rated movie
   - ❑ Get into trouble with my friends
   - ❑ Have sex with someone
   - ❑ Turn on the TV
   - ❑ Yell at my girlfriend or boyfriend
   - ❑ Wear something different
   - ❑ Dye my hair
   - ❑ Have a few beers
   - ❑ Get an attitude
   - ❑ Smoke cigarettes or chew tobacco
   - ❑ Talk with God
   - ❑ Fight with one of my parents
   - ❑ Blow off my schoolwork
   - ❑ Other—

2. What do you think? **Y (yes), N (no),** or **M (maybe)**?
   - ___ The music I listen to encourages rebellion.
   - ___ Rebellion is a sin.
   - ___ No one has the right to tell anyone else what to do.
   - ___ If my friends rebel, then I do too.
   - ___ Rebellion was a 1970s thing—it doesn't apply today.
   - ___ Christians can rebel in their own ways too.
   - ___ Seeking personal happiness leads to rebellion.
   - ___ There's a lot to rebel against in today's society.
   - ___ Young people do what adults and authorities tell them.
   - ___ Christ was a rebel.
   - ___ Rebellion can sometimes be a good thing.

3. On the scale below, place an X where you see yourself.

   Livin' on the edge • Rebellious, but not crazy • Occasionally rebellious • Me? Rebellious? No way.

4. How would you answer these questions?

   In what ways should Christians **rebel**?

   In what ways should Christians **not rebel**?

5. Which of the following stories in the Bible describe **godly rebellion** and which describes **sinful rebellion**?
   Exodus 32:1-4 (Aaron and the golden calf)
   Jonah 3 (Jonah's witness)
   Malachi 3:6, 7 (Relationship of God's people to God)
   Matthew 2:9-12 (The magi and King Herod)
   Acts 4:32-35 (Early church believers)

From *More High School TalkSheets—Updated!* by David Lynn. Permission to reproduce this page granted only for use in the buyer's own youth group. www.YouthSpecialties.com

THIS WEEK

Teenagers are often seen as disobedient, stubborn, uncooperative, delinquent, oppositional, and defiant—all words that can describe some aspect of rebellion. Some people think that rebellion in the adolescent years is normal and expected. That's not true. Most teenagers don't rebel. They buy into the cultural values that exist within their communities. But some teenagers do rebel—and get into some serious trouble. It's every parent's worst nightmare, and for some it's a reality. This TalkSheet provides the opportunity to discuss both the good and the bad aspects of rebellion with your students.

OPENER

You may want to start by having your kids make a list of all the things that they or their peers do to rebel. What do kids their age do to rebel? You may get a wide variety of answers—some more serious than others. Write all the suggestions down on a whiteboard or poster board. Then ask your group to rate these from 1 to 10 (1 being "not really a big deal" and 10 being "really serious"). Now ask them which one is most common among kids their age. Why do some kids rebel more than others? And why do some kids do worse things than others?

Where do kids learn to rebel? Ask your group to name the influences that encourage rebellion. TV shows? Older brothers or sisters? Celebrities? Professional athletes? Musicians? Movies? Listening to music? What are these influences and why are some stronger than others? How does exposure to the media relate to rebellion (for example, do those who listen to violent music rebel more than others)?

THE DISCUSSION, BY NUMBERS

1. You've most likely covered this question if you used the suggested opener. Widen the discussion by asking your students when they usually feel the most rebellious and why. What triggers kids to rebel sometimes more than others? Why are some kids more rebellious than others?

2. Take some time to talk about each of these statements. What do your kids think of rebellion? What about Christians who rebel?

3. Some of your kids may not want to tell where they are on this scale. You may want to ask where teenagers in general would put themselves on the scale. What about Christian teenagers?

4. Ask the group if they think they're rebelling in Christian ways—or if they're conforming to the influences of society. What arguments to they have for either case? Do they think God sees rebellion as a good thing or a bad thing?

5. You may want to talk about each story you're your group. What does God say about rebellion? How does each of the Bible stories relate to rebellion today?

THE CLOSE

Summarize the discussion by pointing out the two types of rebellion—godly and sinful. Everyone has rebelled against God in his or her own ways. No one is perfect because everyone sins against God. But God provided a way back to him through the sacrifice of his son, Jesus. (Romans 5:6-8; Ephesians 2:14-18). Christians—as followers of Christ—are called to rebel against the sinful pattern of the world and to conform to the image of Christ (James 4:4). How do Christians rebel today? What about Christian teenagers today? How can your kids become bold and very strong (Philemon 1:8) in their faith? Where is the line between sinful rebellion and godly rebellion? How would they define the two in their own words?

MORE

● Where do your kids learn rebellion or see it in the media and in society? Go back to question 1 above and ask your kids to list all the TV shows, movies, advertisements, music songs, and other places where they see, hear, experience, or learn about rebellion. What about godly rebellion? Is that condoned in the same way that sinful rebellion is? Why or why not? Have your kids keep their eyes open during the week for rebellion around them. Where did they see it and what happened?

● You may want to look at some Bible characters who were rebels for God—and spoke up for their faith, followed their beliefs, and served their God. A few examples include Esther (who stood up to her husband—the king), Mary (who was pregnant with Jesus—when she was still a virgin), Paul (a big rebel—who eventually died because of it), and more. Have your kids look through the Bible stories to look at the characters. How did these people rebel against others for God?

BRAVE NEW WORLD

1. What are **three hopes** and **dreams** that you have for the future?

2. Put an X on the scale below in the area that best describes your outlook about your **personal future**.

Very bright   Totally bleak

Place an X on the scale below in the area that best describes your outlook about the **future of the church**.

Very bright   Totally bleak

Place an X on the scale below in the area that best describes your outlook toward the **future of the country**.

Very bright   Totally bleak

3. Put an arrow by the items you think will be the **top three problems** for the world in the future.

Crime	Selfishness	Energy crisis
Friction between generations	Violence	Animal and plant extinction
Poverty	Child abuse	Economic depression
Drug abuse	Global warming	Sexually transmitted
Racism	Environmental pollution	diseases
War	Pornography on the	Homosexuality
Sexual or physical abuse	Internet	Corruption and dishonesty
Decline in moral values	Increase in the occult or	Rape
Divorce or family fighting	New Age religions	Other—

4. What does God have to offer for **your future**?

5. What can you do to influence the future for **Christ**?

6. Check out one of the following passages from the Bible—what does it have to say about the future?

Proverbs 19:21   1 Corinthians 13:12
Luke 12:16-20   James 4:13-17

From *More High School TalkSheets—Updated!* by David Lynn. Permission to reproduce this page granted only for use in the buyer's own youth group. www.YouthSpecialties.com

BRAVE NEW WORLD [the future]

THIS WEEK

The future holds a lot for the young people of today. Some have mixed feelings about it—maybe some are worried about the economy or moral standards, while some are just concerned about their personal lives and what will happen to them. This TalkSheet offers an opportunity to discuss the future, its hopes and dreams—and promise of hope that Christ gives Christians for the future.

OPENER

This activity works as an opener, but is also a good way for your students to get to know each other better. Pass out paper and pens to everyone and then ask your kids to take a couple of minutes to describe how they see themselves in 10 years. Remind them not to give their identities away, but to make their predictions as realistic as possible. Afterwards collect the descriptions and read them aloud one at a time. After you read each one, ask the group to guess the identity of the person. Then take a vote and let the group come to a consensus about whose future seems to be the most accurate and why. Why did the person describe why they see their future that way? You may want to talk about how setting goals ties in with the future. How does setting goals affect one's future?

THE DISCUSSION, BY NUMBERS

1. You may want to your kids and keep track of their answers on the board, then take note of the most common hopes among the group. Why do they hope for these things in their lives? How do they think their non-Christian friends would answer? Would they have the same hopes? Are the dreams of Christians any different from the dreams of those who aren't? Should they be different?

2. Some kids view their futures as brighter than others. Others rate their personal futures brighter than the country's. Talk about why there is a difference. Focus on how the group feels it can influence the church positively and thus influence the country on behalf of Christ.

3. What problems do your kids see in the future? Why did they choose the problems they did? You may want to spend some time talking about why some problems are more of a threat than others. See if you can reach a group consensus about the top three problems.

4. Many young people believe that economic prosperity will be their security for the future. Contrast this with the Bible's message, which points to a relationship with Christ as the only hope for the future.

5. Some kids think—based on TV or movies—that everyone has the right to a happy and financially secure future. Spend some time talking about the future for Christians and what your kids can do to make the future better.

6. What did these verses say to your group? You may want to go through each one and talk about how it relates to the future.

THE CLOSE

God is the God of the past, the present, and the future. He's in control of eternity! In serving God, people may not know the future, but because they know the God of the future, they can be confident that it will all work out according to God's plan (Romans 8:28). Sometimes the future is uncertain and scary, and things don't always go smoothly. That doesn't mean God doesn't love his children. It means he gives each person unique trials and challenges to bring them closer to him and make them stronger in their faith.

You may want to go back to the most common hope of the students. Was it their relationship with Christ? Challenge the group to hope and work toward a serious commitment to Christ both today and tomorrow. After all, what sort of future would they have without him?

MORE

● You may want to choose a problem from question 3 and decide how the group can make a difference for Christ in that area—right now. You may want to brainstorm with your group and come up with a fundraiser or group activity, such as visiting a homeless shelter, contributing money to an organization, or simply committing to pray for a problem in the world. Give your kids tangible ideas of what they can do and then remind them that they can make a difference through the small things—letting God work through them to make a difference.

● Encourage your kids to make a list of their goals, hopes, and dreams for the future. Have them make a list of 10 things that they'd like to do within the next 10 years. How about within their lifetime? You may want to let them share these items with the group. Challenge them to pray about each of these goals and dreams. How can God help them achieve these? How tangible are their goals? Why or why not? Why are setting goals and challenging oneself important?

CREATION CANCELLATION

1. Do you know someone who has had an **abortion**? (Please don't share any names!)

2. What do you think about the following statements?
Do you **SA (strongly agree)**, **A (agree)**, **D (disagree)**, or **SD (strongly disagree)**?

___ A woman legally has a right to determine what she does with her body.

___ Life begins at conception.

___ Abortion is murder—it's killing a human being.

___ A father should have some say in a mother's decision to have an abortion.

___ Safe, legal abortions are better than dangerous, illegal abortions.

___ Abortion is an easy out for those who aren't responsible when having sex.

___ Abortion is a necessary evil.

___ Since there aren't specific guidelines in the Bible regarding abortion, Christians shouldn't worry about it.

___ The availability of the morning-after pill (RU 486) should be restricted.

___ Abortion is all right for others, but I don't believe in it myself.

3. What do you think—are any of these legitimate cases for abortion? **Y (yes)** or **N (no)**?
Abortion should be available for the following—

___ A pregnant 12-year-old

___ A woman expecting a baby with a mental or physical handicap

___ A drug-addicted mother

___ A pregnant 26-year-old single career woman

___ A woman whose health is threatened by the pregnancy

___ A woman who already has more than six children

___ A woman or adolescent who is pregnant as a result of rape or incest

___ An AIDS-infected pregnant woman

___ A pregnant mother on welfare

___ No one should have an abortion

4. What do you think each of these verses has to say about abortion?
Genesis 1:27
Exodus 20:13
Job 10:8-12
Psalm 139:13-16

From *More High School TalkSheets—Updated!* by David Lynn. Permission to reproduce this page granted only for use in the buyer's own youth group. www.YouthSpecialties.com

CREATION CANCELLATION [abortion]

THIS WEEK

Abortion is a controversial and hotly debated topic. Two clearly defined camps do battle daily over this issue—the pro-choice and the pro-life movements. Most Americans fall somewhere in between because they have mixed feelings about abortion. This TalkSheet provides your group with a structured opportunity to debate the abortion issue, and what the Bible has to say about it.

You may want to be cautious of your church's stance on abortion and birth control before you start this discussion. Some churches are more sensitive to discussing these issues than others. Also, be extra sensitive to any kids in your group who may be sexually active. Be careful not to sound judgmental or condemning—try to keep an open attitude for an open discussion.

OPENER

For this opener, place two chairs opposite each other in front of the group. Then hang a sign on the back of each chair so the group can see them—one sign says PRO-LIFE and the other should say PRO-CHOICE. Give your kids some case scenarios, like the ones listed below. Then let your kids take turns debating the situations and the issues. The person who is talking on each side must sit in the chair. Be sure that everyone gets a chance to sit in the chair and speak. When each person has made his or her argument, let someone else tag-team him or her to debate and so on. Continue this until you feel the group has had a good debate and then continue into the TalkSheet.
•Alexa and Trevor have been having sex for a while. Now Alexa is pregnant. Trevor thinks that Alexa has the right to choose what to do with her body.
•Shani has a rare and serious blood disorder that would put her at great risk if she tried to give birth. She is pregnant and now her doctor has recommended an abortion to her and her husband.
•Courtney has been a victim of a date rape situation. She feels ashamed, confused, and really scared. She never expected this to happen and now she is pregnant.
•Maria has had in-vitro fertilization and the doctors have fertilized five eggs in her uterus. Now they say she should get rid of three in order to have a better chance of having two implanted for pregnancy.

THE DISCUSSION, BY NUMBERS

1. How many of your kids answered yes? Be very sensitive when discussing this issue—some of your students may have had abortions or had girlfriends who had one.

2. No other subject creates a more heated debate than the issue of abortion. Because the issue involves fundamental beliefs, it's easy to become judgmental of those with opposing viewpoints. Let the students express their honest opinions. Mediate the discussion and save your comments for the end.

3. This activity focuses on one of the fundamental issues of this debate—the circumstances and the reasons behind the need for an abortion. Let your students share their answers and help categorize each reason as soft or hard. Talk with the group about the ministry opportunities that may result from crisis pregnancies.

4. What are your kids' interpretations of these Bible verses as they relate to the issue of abortion? What does God say about the issue of abortion?

THE CLOSE

Wrap up by talking about the views of your group and those of your church. Take a biblical look at both the reasons for abortion and how these relate to the world and today's teenagers. What are the ramifications of having an abortion? What are the pros and cons of having one or not having one?

Also, remind your kids that God is compassionate. If they or someone they know has had an abortion, encourage them to find a trusted adult to talk with.

MORE

● Most communities have agencies or representatives that advocate pro-life or pro-choice agendas. You may want to have some of your kids get some materials from both of these, review these materials, and report back to the group what they learned. What does each say about abortion? How are they different? What alternatives does each of them give?

● If you'd like to direction your students to some informative sites on abortion and adoption, check out Adopt (www.adopting.org/ar.html), Bethany Christian Services (www.bethany.org), Healing Hearts Ministries (www.healinghearts.org), Pregnancy Centers Online (www.pregnancycenters.org), Prolife.org (www.prolife.org), or the Ultimate Pro-life Resource List (www.prolifeinfo.org).

HELP WANTED

1. What do you think of this statement? Check a box in each column.
Teenagers lack the knowledge and experience necessary to have a meaningful ministry with others.
   - ❏ Most adults believe this.
   - ❏ Some adults believe this.
   - ❏ Hardly any adults believe this.
   - ❏ Most teenagers believe this.
   - ❏ Some teenagers believe this.
   - ❏ Hardly any teenagers believe this.

2. Do you **A (agree)** or **D (disagree)** with the following statements?
   - ___ High schoolers should think of themselves before they think of others.
   - ___ Teenagers are powerless to make the world a better place.
   - ___ If teenagers were paid well, they would help the poor, the hungry, or the homeless.
   - ___ Serving others through volunteer work helps teenagers become more successful adults.
   - ___ Teenagers would rather be entertained by the church than challenged to help others.
   - ___ If teenagers want to be more like Jesus, they need to serve others in his name.

3. What do you think is the **biggest obstacle** standing in the way of teenagers helping others in the name of Christ?

4. If you could pick and plan **one service project** to take part in, what would you do?

5. Check out what these verses say about Christian service.

Psalm 34:14	Luke 6:35	James 2:17
Habakkuk 1:2-5	1 Corinthians 9:19	1 Peter 2:12
Matthew 5:16	Philippians 2:4	
Matthew 25:34-40	1 Timothy 6:18, 19	

From *More High School TalkSheets—Updated!* by David Lynn. Permission to reproduce this page granted only for use in the buyer's own youth group. www.YouthSpecialties.com

HELP WANTED [Christian service]

THIS WEEK

Christian service is an important part of being in the church. But today, some adults think that youth groups are more concerned about camps and fun activities. But teenagers have a lot to give. This TalkSheet helps you to focus your group's attention on the opportunities that await Christians willing to serve the Lord.

OPENER

For this opener, bring several days' worth of newspapers to your youth meeting and break the students into small groups. Give each group some of the papers and tell them to look for articles that identify a need in your community. Each group should then pick one article from those they found and present the article to the rest of the group, defining the need and possible solutions or resources that could help meet this need. Keep track of the problems and solutions from each group on the whiteboard or overhead. After every group has presented, have them come together to discuss the viability and reality of the proposed solutions. Could the youth group help meet these needs and make a difference in your community? This challenge is a great lead-in to the discussion.

THE DISCUSSION, BY NUMBERS

1. Why do some people think teenagers aren't consulted and utilized more in community and Christian service? How does that make your kids feel? Why do some people have this misconception?

2. Poll the answers to each of the statements. What do your kids think? Have them share their opinions and debate if they don't agree. Discuss the pros and cons of each statement.

3. What's standing in their way in getting out there in the name of Christ? Allow the young people to volunteer their completed sentences with the group. How can they get rid of these obstacles?

4. Ask the group to share their ideas (you can split them in groups to brainstorm if you want). How easily could a project like this be planned and what are the benefits of participating this project? Make a master list of their ideas and discuss the ones that would be the most accessible for your group.

5. Create a master list of what the group learned about Christian service. Focus on two or three of the passages for group discussion.

THE CLOSE

Christ was and is the transformer of society. Sin in the world affects more than just individuals—it affects all of society. But because of Christ, people are free from sin and are called to work for the good of mankind (Titus 2:7; 3:8) to show the love of Jesus to others. Emphasize that your kids—and all Christians—have a responsibility as God's children to care for those around us—for both their physical and emotional needs. You may want to close by reading Matthew 25:31-46 and with a time of prayer.

MORE

- What can your kids do to make a difference for others? You may want to plan a service project for your group, based on their interests in helping others. For more ideas of what your group can do for missions or service projects, check out *Ideas Library: Camps, Retreats, Missions & Service Ideas for Youth Groups* (Youth Specialties).

- Why do a lot of people not like to help others? How has today's self-centered society corrupted the desire to help others? You may want to take a look at how the media and society have influenced people to become more self-centered and less Christ-centered. What influence do advertisements and commercials have on people? Why is society focused more on money than on loving others? What can your kids do to avoid getting caught in the self-centered trap?

TOP OF THE LIST

1. What is the absolute, number one, biggest, **most important priority** in your life?

2. Imagine for a minute that your life priorities could not exceed a certain point value. You, as a teenager, have 50 points total. How will you use them? Pick the items from the list below for a total of 50 points.

Six points each—
Having a job
Being a disciple of Christ
Having a good time
Improving my looks
Wearing the right clothes
Studying hard
Spending time on the Internet
Owning a car
Being a leader in the church

Five points each—
Attending church regularly
Consistently participating in youth group
Telling others about Christ
Volunteering to help others
Staying active in sports
Regularly studying the Bible
Having a boyfriend or girlfriend

Four points each—
Watching music videos
Turning homework in on time
Helping other teenagers
Buying music CDs
Working on musical talent
Playing video or computer games
Participating in extracurricular activities

Three points each—
Keeping a best friend
Going out on Saturday nights
Getting along with parents
Spending time with friends
Staying in shape
Seeing the latest movies

Two points each—
Remaining alcohol and drug free
Having Christian friends
Praying every day

One point each—
Watching television
Getting to class on time
Reading magazines

3. How do you think your priorities will change in the **next two years**?

4. Which do you think is worse—God not being a priority in someone's life or God being a low priority in someone's life?

   ❑ God not a priority at all   ❑ God low on the priority list

5. Check out these verses and finish these statements in your own words.
   Proverbs 3:6 When your priorities recognize God, then—
   Titus 1:16 My actions reflect that my priority is—
   Revelation 3:14-18 Choose God's priorities because otherwise—

From *More High School TalkSheets—Updated!* by David Lynn. Permission to reproduce this page granted only for use in the buyer's own youth group. www.YouthSpecialties.com

TOP OF THE LIST [priorities]

THIS WEEK

This TalkSheet takes an honest look at young people's priorities. In a culture that pulls young people in all directions, take time to help your kids see why God needs to be in the center of their lives and priorities.

OPENER

To start, give you kids a list of different tasks they may have to do on a given day. You can either hand this list out to individual groups or write the list on a whiteboard or poster board. A few examples can include things like—

• Going to bed on time (getting enough sleep)
• Taking a shower or bath
• Eating three meals a day
• Helping your mom or dad out around the house
• Doing your homework
• Going to basketball (or whatever sport) practice
• Spending some time with God
• Talking with your boyfriend or girlfriend
• Getting up on time in the morning
• Hanging with your friends
• Exercising to keep yourself healthy
• Checking your e-mail or surfing the Internet
• Going shopping for new clothes or other stuff

Go ahead and add whatever other things you'd like to add. Now ask your kids to prioritize this list from 1 to 12 (12 being the most important thing on this list). If you split your group into smaller groups, ask each group to share their prioritized list. Then, come to a consensus with the whole group. How did your kids decide which was most important? Least important? How might these priorities change as they get older? What priorities may be added in the future? Use this activity as a springboard for discussion on priorities.

THE DISCUSSION, BY NUMBERS

1. What's on the absolute top of your students' lists? You may want to make a list of them for the group to see. Challenge the students to look at what they really like to spend their time doing.

2. Ask several group members to describe the priorities they selected with their 50 points. Concentrate the discussion on which priorities most kids picked and how they made their choices. Ask if the relative point values given to the various priorities were accurate—which would they have assigned more points? Or fewer points?

3. Begin the discussion of this item by first examining how the students' priorities have changed in the last two years. Include a review of where they placed God in their priorities. Then examine the

upcoming two years, again including where God will fit into their future priorities. Get very specific with examples from kids' lives.

4. Some young people may say that this is not a fair question, but it is a reality. Which statement hits home closest to your kids? How can God can be moved from a low priority to a number one priority?

5. This activity contrasts the world's view of priorities with God's view. Each passage views God as the beginning and the end of priorities. Point out the sharp contrast between what the Bible says and what the world says. Have the students share their completed sentences.

THE CLOSE

Point out to your group that priorities can be easy to set but hard to live out. But what's most important is what's on their hearts—what really matters to them and what God puts on their hearts. Matthew 6:21 says "For where your priorities are, there your heart will be also" (author's paraphrase). As your kids live their daily priorities out, these priorities will become etched on their hearts. And God will work in their hearts to show them what's really important. Challenge your kids to examine their priorities. What would honor and serve God the most? How can your kids being to re-prioritize their lives? How can being close to God make it easier to figure out their priorities? Close with a time of prayer, asking God to show you and your kids his priorities for them.

MORE

● Have a New Year's in July—or whatever month you are using this TalkSheet! Break the young people up into groups of three or four. Ask them to write down some resolutions in the form of priorities they would like to keep. Have them share their lists with those in their group for the purpose of accountability in the coming weeks and months.

● What does society say about priorities? You may want to have your kids pay attention to the media this week—particularly TV advertisements, commercials, and magazine ads. What do these ads say about prioritizing and getting what you want? What do TV shows say about what's most important? Take some time to talk about these with your group and have them bring in some examples. Then ask them this question—how does the media influence our priorities? And what can they do to keep their priorities straight when the media says different things?

DO CHEATERS PROSPER?

1. Estimate the percentage of students at your school who you think frequently cheat.

2. Rank the following reasons high school students cheat from **best (1)** to **worst (10)**.
___ Laziness
___ Lost their notes or book
___ Not enough time to study
___ Pressure to get good grades
___ Afraid of failing
___ Need to graduate
___ Competition for college entrance
___ Everybody else does it
___ Not liking the specific class
___ Forgot about the test or quiz

3. Which of these statements do you think is the **most true**?
❑ Guys cheat more than girls.
❑ Adults cheat in life as much as students cheat in school.
❑ Non-Christians cheat more than Christians.
❑ Cheating is worth the risks.
❑ There are times when a student has to cheat.

4. Is it cheating? Read each of the following statements and decide, then answer with **S (seriously cheating)**, **B (barely cheating)**, or **N (not really cheating)**.
___ a. Copying off of someone's test paper.
___ b. Writing answers on your arm or hand for a test.
___ c. Allowing your parent to do a homework assignment.
___ d. Asking someone sitting near you for the answer to a test question.
___ e. Copying someone else's book report from last year.
___ f. Letting a friend copy answers from your test.
___ g. Telling a friend an answer to a test question.
___ h. Letting another student help you on a special project.
___ i. Letting someone copy an answer from your homework.
___ j. Copying an answer from someone else's homework.
___ k. Changing an answer for someone when papers are exchanged for grading purposes.
___ l. Asking someone to change an answer for you when papers are exchanged for grading purposes.
___ m. Taking information straight off the Internet when you're writing a paper.

5. Check out **Proverbs 1:10-19**. What does this say about cheating and its consequences?

DO CHEATERS PROSPER? [cheating]

THIS WEEK

To cheat or not to cheat—it's a moral issue young people must face every day. The high school experience provides many chances to cheat. From homework to papers to tests, students have to wrestle with honesty decisions—and many of these decisions aren't always clear-cut. Use this TalkSheet to examine the different aspects of cheating and how a Christian student can cope.

OPENER

How does it feel when a person is cheated on? Well, try this activity with your kids. Split your group up into two groups of "cheaters" and "non-cheaters." Have your kids draw pieces of paper from a hat—on some pieces put a star (or some other sign) and the rest leave blank. Then ask all the kids with stars on their papers to come to the front. Take them into a different area and explain to them that they are the cheaters. (You may want to have just a few kids in your group be the cheaters, depending on the size of your group.) Their job is to cheat as much as possible during the upcoming game without giving themselves away to the other group. Then give them a cheat sheet—a list of answers to the trivia game (or any other game that you want to play). Remind them to be as unobvious as possible.

Next, play a game of Bible trivia (or your game of choice) with your kids. Tell the group that the person who comes up with the most correct answers wins a free lunch at your expense. Then pass out a list of questions to each of your kids to answer. (You can either pick out some questions beforehand or check out www.Biblequizzes.com or www.bible-triv-ia.com.) Go through the answers after a few minutes. Have your kids keep track of the questions they got right. Who got the most questions correct? What were the reactions of some kids who didn't get many right as opposed to those who already had the answers? After some discussion time, tell your group that there were some kids who already had the answers—and no, they don't get a free lunch, because they cheated. Use this activity to springboard into a discussion about cheating and how it feels to be cheated on and to cheat.

THE DISCUSSION, BY NUMBERS

1. What percentage of high schoolers did your kids guess? Write down their responses and compare them. Why is there a lot of, or not much, cheating? What gripes do your kids have about cheaters?

2. These are some of the common excuses students give themselves for cheating. Rank these excuses as a group. Why do some work better than others?

3. What do your kids think about these statements? Why are some true or false? Take some time to talk about these with your group.

4. What exactly is cheating? Each of these statements is a cheating situation—some are active cheating (seeking to cheat for your own grade) while others are passive cheating (allowing others to use you for the sake of their grade). Once you've debated each statement, talk about passive and active cheating and point out that both are examples of cheating because both are deceptive, dishonest, and against most school rules.

5. What does this verse say about cheating? As a group, come up with a definition of cheating.

THE CLOSE

Explain that cheating is stealing—and it gives one an illusion of power and control. Cheating is a form of a lying, and usually one lie piles onto another until the person gets caught. Cheating does catch up to a person eventually. Why is cheating a temptation? How does Satan use cheating to pull Christians away from God? Challenge your kids to trust themselves and to do the right thing.

MORE

● Have the students decide whether or not they agree with the title of this TalkSheet—do cheaters prosper? Is the saying "cheaters never prosper" valid or invalid? Ask the group to list additional examples of young people cheating—cheating on boyfriends or girlfriends, on friends, on parents, and so on. Are these other forms of cheating prosperous? Why do people have an illusion that cheating can make you prosperous?

● Do your kids think that society or the media condones cheating? Why or why not? How does the "get ahead" mentality influence cheating and stealing? What are the stiff penalties for getting caught cheating? Do your kids know what happens in a college or university if someone is caught cheating or plagiarizing something that's not theirs? See what your kids know or can find out—encourage them to ask, call, or e-mail their teachers, local high schools, and colleges.

SATAN & CO.

1. Write down the first thing that comes to mind when you hear the word **Satan**.

2. How much **truth** do you think there is in movies and TV shows that depict Satan and demons?

3. Rate the following activities on a scale of 1 (Satan has little involvement in it) to 14 (Satan is very involved in it).

    ___ Dating
    ___ Movies
    ___ A Christian's daily life
    ___ Drug use
    ___ Halloween
    ___ Ministry and the church
    ___ Suicide

    ___ The Internet
    ___ Violent or vulgar music
    ___ Astrology
    ___ Fashion
    ___ Homosexuality
    ___ Wicca or New Age religions
    ___ Politics and government

4. How involved are teenagers at your school in each of the following? **V (very involved)**, **K (kind of involved)** or **U (uninvolved)**?

    ___ Horoscopes
    ___ Tarot-card reading
    ___ Wearing satanic symbols
    ___ Ouija board playing
    ___ Fantasy role-playing games
    ___ Magic
    ___ Novels with occult themes

    ___ Witchcraft/Wicca
    ___ Séances
    ___ Crystals
    ___ Spirit guides
    ___ Psychic hotlines
    ___ Other—

5. Do you **A (agree)** or **D (disagree)** with each of these statements?

    ___ Satanic involvement is a trend for today's teenagers.
    ___ Satan and demons are the creation of superstitious imaginations.
    ___ God will one day crush Satan because Jesus conquered sin and death.
    ___ Dabbling in the satanic (Ouija boards, tarot cards, and so on) is relatively harmless.
    ___ The satanic themes found in some hard-core music are gimmicks to increase sales.
    ___ Christians don't take Satan and his demonic influence on them seriously enough.
    ___ A Christian can be attacked by demons.
    ___ Satan can't get near you if you are God's child.

6. Based on the verses below, how can Christians can stand against Satan?
   Ephesians 6:10-18   1 Peter 5:8, 9   James 4:7

From *More High School TalkSheets—Updated!* by David Lynn. Permission to reproduce this page granted only for use in the buyer's own youth group. www.YouthSpecialties.com

SATAN & CO. [satanism]

THIS WEEK

Too many times talking about the satanic will spark curiosity in kids and the next thing you know, they're logging onto every satanic Web site on the Internet for more information. The discussion that takes place shouldn't focus on the gory details of satanic rituals and worship, but addresses the realities of satanic involvement by today's high school youth—and the dangers of getting involved.

OPENER

You may want to ask your group members to name all of the movies or TV shows that contain demonic or satanic themes. You may want to make a list of these for all to see (you may be able to learn a thing or two!). Point out the growing trend in our culture toward the satanic. How should Christians react to this? Why do your kids think there is such an interest in the demonic? Are these movies or shows good for Christians to see? Why or why not? How about other people and non-Christians? Do these TV shows or movies make light of the spiritual dimension? Why or why not?

Or read to your group the story of Christ and Satan in the desert (Matthew 4:1-11). What does this story say about Satan and his power? How did he try to trick Jesus?

THE DISCUSSION, BY NUMBERS

1. Write the word *Satan* on the whiteboard or poster board. Ask the students to list all of their responses. What is the most common thought about Satan? Where do they get this idea?

2. On a whiteboard or poster board, place two headings—fact and fiction—with a vertical line drawn between them. Brainstorm a list of truths about Satan under the fact heading and a list of false ideas about Satan under the fiction heading.

3. You can expect a wide range of answers on this. Give your kids time to debate their responses.

4. Again you can expect a wide range of answers on this. The objective is to find out to what extent satanism is a problem. Follow up with a question like this, "Why do you think satanism is a growing phenomenon?"

5. Have the students share their opinions on each one and give reasons why they feel the way they do. See if the group can come to a consensus regarding Satan's influence on today's high schoolers.

6. You may want to divide your kids into small groups and have each group take a different passage of the Bible.

THE CLOSE

Point out that one of Satan's strategies is to convince people that he doesn't exist. The other strategy is to convince people he is real and can provide them with power. That's appealing to some young people—especially those who feel powerless and who don't know the truth. Only the one true God has the power for living, fills people with joy and peace, and loves them unconditionally.

Emphasize the reality of Satan and the evil work he and his demons are carrying out in today's world. This can be effectively and quickly done by pointing out some of the names the Bible has given Satan—Tempter (Matthew 4:3), Liar (John 8:44), Enemy (1 Peter 5:8), Evil One (1 John 5:19), and Accuser (Revelation 12:10). Also emphasize that Christ came to destroy the work of the Devil (1 John 3:8), and that Christ—who dwells in every Christian through the Holy Spirit—is greater than Satan (1 John 4:4).

What's the most powerful tool for protection from Satan? Prayer. Encourage your kids to pray for God's protection and to pray for the leaders in the church, like the pastors, elders, and other leaders. Close with a time of prayer with your group and let your group members know that you are available to pray with them and talk more with them.

MORE

● You may want to read or encourage your kids to check out Frank Peretti's novels on spiritual warfare, including *This Present Darkness*, *Piercing the Darkness*, *The Prophet*, and *The Oath*. These books are fiction novels, but portray the power of Satan and his forces—and the overriding force of prayer from Christians! There are also several other Christian books on spiritual warfare. Be sure to skim over the section you will read so that you can explain to and discuss it with your group.

● Some of your kids may have dabbled in satanism or have friends who have. Take some more time to talk about the dangers of getting involved in this—even for innocent fun. What can your kids do if they or others are hooked on satanism? What can you do to pull them back? For more information, check out Cult Awareness & Information Center (www.caic.org.au), Apologetics Research Resources on Religious Cults, Sects, Movements, Doctrines, Etc. (www.gospelcom.net/apologeticsindex), or www.YouthSpecialties.com for more links.

THE HITS

1. What do you think most adults think about secular music?

2. Where do you stand? Check the one that fits you the best.
   - ❑ I listen to secular music because I like how it sounds.
   - ❑ Listening to music puts me in a better mood.
   - ❑ I listen to music to fit in with my peers and friends.
   - ❑ Music is just part of our culture and society.
   - ❑ The lyrics of music don't affect me.

3. What do you think? Do you **A (agree)** or **D (disagree)** with these statements?
   - ___ There's more good than bad in secular music.
   - ___ Secular concerts should be rated like movies.
   - ___ The lyrics of music have less influence on teens than critics believe.
   - ___ Sometimes secular music is inspired by Satan.
   - ___ Popular music continues to get worse morally.
   - ___ Young people identify who they are by the groups they listen to.
   - ___ Adults shouldn't protect kids from secular music.
   - ___ Freedom of speech guarantees artists the right to sing whatever they want to sing.
   - ___ Music has little power to change the world.
   - ___ Music artists are accountable only to themselves.
   - ___ Music is a good source of information about life.

4. At what point should parents become concerned about their kid's involvement in secular music?

5. Name five popular songs that you hear on the radio or on CD. Then rate the lyrics for a Christian, using the following scale: **A (acceptable), H (harmless), Q (questionable), U (unhealthy/sinful)**.

6. Check out **John 17:15-19**. How do these Bible verses relate to the world of popular music? Why or why not?

From *More High School TalkSheets—Updated!* by David Lynn. Permission to reproduce this page granted only for use in the buyer's own youth group. www.YouthSpecialties.com

THE HITS [popular music]

THIS WEEK

Whether it is hip-hop, alternative, country, or rap, *music* is one word that defines youth culture today. It's become a medium targeted specifically at teenagers, who purchase over 125 million CDs a year*. But popular music—and the world it has created—has little or nothing to do with the home or church. Your high schoolers have already established listening habits. This TalkSheet has been designed to create a positive dialogue about popular, secular music between students and adult youth workers.

OPENER

Ask your group how music plays a role in everyday life. It's not just something people listen to. Where do your kids see music videos, hear music, or see music? Some of these include TV advertisements, radio commercials, movies, stores, billboards, and more. Discuss how music has invaded culture and what influences it has. For example, what would a movie be like without a soundtrack? What would commercials be without background music? Why do stores play music while you're shopping?

Have your kids make a list of all their favorite music groups and performers. Write these down on a master list. How have the kids tell you what genre of music these are—Pop? Rock? Alternative? Swing? Jazz? Techno? Country? Christian? Point out to your group that today there isn't as clear of a line as there used to be between popular music and Christian music. Christian artists have crossed over mainstream, while mainstream bands have Christian musicians in them. What groups do your kids know that have Christian members?

THE DISCUSSION, BY NUMBERS

1. How do kids feel about their parents and music? Are their parents strict? Nosy? Uninterested? How does this affect kids and the music they listen to? What do their parents think is the effect of their attitudes toward their kids' music?

2. Where do your kids stand? Most don't think that their music affects them in negative ways. But it does. Point out how music has had an adverse effect on its listeners. Then make a list of positive things about music as well as negative.

3. You may want to ask your kids to pick five or six statements they would like to discuss. You may also want to question what messages secular music sends.

4. Encourage your kids to let their parents into their world—that includes their CDs and radio stations. Discuss all the objections students might have about talking with their parents about music. What objections might parents have to talking with their kids about music?

5. Encourage your kids to be discerning with the music they listen to. You may want to ask students to bring specific songs to play, so they can discuss as a group how each should be rated.

6. Discuss how music influences the students—how does music influence immorality, sexual behaviors, involvement in drugs and alcohol, abuse, and more? Remind them that Satan is trying to have an impact on them and do anything to get into their lives, even if it's the music they're listening to.

THE CLOSE

Point out that listening to popular music isn't bad. But some of the music is bad—the violent content, sexual themes, and other messages aren't good. Be careful not to slam your kids with Bible verses or bash their favorite music groups. Instead, focus on your kids' responsibility to choose wisely the kinds of music they listen to, and to be discerning. Challenge your kids to choose songs that can keep their faith focused on Jesus and not worldly values.

MORE

● Brainstorm the values that most mainstream songs deal with. What are the themes that most talk about? They include love, drug abuse, violence, romance, suicide, and more. Make a list, then ask your kids to guess what percentage of the music they listen to deals with these topics. On a scale of 1 to 10 (10 being the most applicable), how well does the music they listen to apply to their lives? Do they share the same values and morals that the musicians do? Why or why not? What influence do your kids think this has on them?

● Check out Plugged In magazine at www.family.org/pplace/pi/ (Focus on the Family) for the latest trends in music, TV, and movies. Also, check out www.YouthSpecialties.com for information and links to finding discussion topics and latest news on teen culture.

* Teen Fact Book 2000, Channel One Network: New York, Los Angeles, Chicago. Used by permission.

BLOCKBUSTERS

1. Check the number of **movies** you watch in an average month at home and the theater.
   - ❑ Fewer than five
   - ❑ Between six and 10
   - ❑ Between 11 and 20
   - ❑ More than 20

2. What types of movies do you **most frequently watch** at home or at the theater? Circle your top three choices.

Adventure	Sports	Musical
Family	Comedy	Western
Science fiction	Horror	Documentary
Action	Classic black and white	
Cartoon	Blood and gore	
Romance	Drama	

3. Re-rate two movies you think may have been inaccurately rated.

   Movie Rating Guidelines
   G (General Audience)
   PG (Parental Guidance Suggested)
   PG-13 (Parent Caution)
   R (Restricted)
   NC-17 (No One Under 17 Admitted)

   Movie: _____   Movie: _____
   Was rated: _____   Was rated: _____
   Should have been rated: _____   Should have been rated: _____

4. List **two values** that you think today's movies teach (such as "all dating relationships involve sex", or "everything ends up okay in the end", and so on).

5. Would you or have you done any of the following below? **Y (yes)** or **N (no)**?
   ___ I walk out of the theater if a movie is inappropriate.
   ___ I turn off a movie at home if it's inappropriate.
   ___ I carefully choose the movies I watch.
   ___ I won't watch a rental video with my friends if it's inappropriate.
   ___ I watch R-rated movies.
   ___ I talk with my parents about the movies I watch.
   ___ I pray about the movies I watch.

6. Read the following four passages from Romans. How does each relate to watching movies.
   Romans 6:12-14   Romans 12:2
   Romans 8:5-8   Romans 14:1-4

From *More High School TalkSheets—Updated!* by David Lynn. Permission to reproduce this page granted only for use in the buyer's own youth group. www.YouthSpecialties.com

BLOCKBUSTERS [movies]

THIS WEEK

Cable, VHS, and DVD movies give high schoolers the chance to watch nearly anything—whatever they want, whenever they want. This TalkSheet provides you with the opportunity to talk about the kinds of movies your group members are viewing and to encourage them to discern what they watch. Since most late high schoolers can legally watch R-rated movies, you won't be able to use that legal rule as a point of persuasion. But you can discuss the pros and cons of healthy and unhealthy movies, and how to make good decisions about them.

OPENER

Start by getting a list of movies showing in your town from a newspaper of off the Internet. Make a list of all the current movies playing on a poster board or whiteboard. Your kids will most likely know all the titles and may even have seen a few of them. Take a poll to see how many of these movies your kids have seen. Then ask if they can say what each movie is rated. How close do they come? Write the rating next to the movie title. Point out that often people don't even look at the ratings before going to the movie. What are the ratings for? How many of their parents enforce the ratings? Why are certain movies rated the same as others, but have less violent or sexual content?

For information on movies and reviews, check out www.HollywoodJesus.com, Preview Family and Movie Review (www.gospelcom.net/preview), Plugged In Magazine (www.family.org/pplace/pi), Movie Finder (www.moviefinder.com), or Film.Com (www.film.com).

THE DISCUSSION, BY NUMBERS

1. Get a group average for a month. Then let the students estimate how many movies they will have watched by the time they graduate from high school—they'll be surprised to see how much they watch!

2. Ask several students to share their top three movie choices (this will give you an idea of the kinds of movies your group is viewing!). How many of the movies they have watched would pass their parents' approval? Why or why not?

3. This activity will (1) help kids become more aware of the reason for a rating system; (2) help kids discern good from bad moral content; and (3) help kids create their own Christian rating system. Ask the group to create a list of all the reasons for rating a movie NC-17, R, PG-13, PG, and G. You will get answers like violence, foul language, sex, nudity, and so on. Now challenge the kids to create their own rating system in light of Christianity. How would they rate the movies differently?

4. Create a group list of all the young people's responses. (You may want to ask them for examples from specific movies.) Then compare the list to see how many good values are taught versus how many bad values are taught. Ask the students to explain how they can watch movies without being affected by the bad values.

5. After getting the students to share their answers, ask them to go back, look at the list, and decide what changes they would like to make in their movie viewing. What changes are they willing to make, if any? Why or why not?

6. Ask them to read their summaries and describe one thing they learned from the book of Romans about movie viewing.

THE CLOSE

Let the kids know that they do have decisions to make when it comes to going to the theater or watching a movie at home. Just because a movie was made doesn't mean that it should be seen! Challenge your kids to find out about movies before they see them (possibly refer them to one of the sites listed above). And even when they can watch an R-rated movie, talk about the content with your kids. How does watching a lot of violence affect a person? What about a highly sexual movie? Encourage them to be discerning with what they see and to take responsibility for their parent's rules and their own beliefs.

MORE

● You can use movies to teach your youth! Check out *Videos That Teach* by Doug Fields and Eddie James (Youth Specialties). This book includes over 75 teachable movie moments from film classics on over a hundred topics. Also, visit the Web site www.teachwithmovies.org for ideas on teaching with movies.

● Consider going to a movie or watching a video with your kids. Make sure that it's a rating that passes the approval of all parents. Afterwards talk about the movie in light of Christianity and their beliefs. What was the movie about? What message did it give about life, love, happiness, and so on? What good or bad influences could this movie have on others? Why or why not?

THIEF IN THE NIGHT

1. Finish this sentence in your own words. If Christ doesn't return soon, the world will—

2. Why would you **not want** Christ to return yet?
   - ❑ I'd like to finish school.
   - ❑ I have plans for my future.
   - ❑ I'd like to make some money first.
   - ❑ I haven't lived a very good life.
   - ❑ I'm scared by the thought of it.
   - ❑ I need more time to spend with my friends.
   - ❑ I want to get married.
   - ❑ I have family and friends who aren't Christians.
   - ❑ I want to have children.
   - ❑ I just started to enjoy life.
   - ❑ I'm not ready.
   - ❑ Other—

3. Do you think that each of these statements is **T (true)** or **F (false)**?
   - ___ The second coming of Christ is one of the most important things taught in the Bible.
   - ___ Christians should spend more time studying biblical prophecy.
   - ___ Differences in beliefs about the second coming of Christ shouldn't divide Christians.
   - ___ Events in the Middle East are exaggerated by Christians as prophetic.
   - ___ There is more evidence than ever before that this is the last generation.
   - ___ Christians are the loners in the world waiting for Christ's return.
   - ___ The future doesn't matter, since the world will end soon anyway.

4. If you knew for certain Christ would return next year, how would you live your life differently?

5. Check out **2 Peter 3:10-13** and complete the following sentence.

   Because Christ will return, Christians should—

From *More High School TalkSheets—Updated!* by David Lynn. Permission to reproduce this page granted only for use in the buyer's own youth group. www.YouthSpecialties.com

THIEF IN THE NIGHT [Christ's return]

THIS WEEK

Many high schoolers are fascinated with the book of Revelation and the end of the world. They want to know about the future and what it holds for them. So many people believed that the year 2000 would be the time of Christ's return—now they've been left disappointed and wondering. What do your kids think about Christ's return? This TalkSheet will let you openly talk about the return of Christ with your group.

OPENER

You may want to start by splitting your group up into smaller groups and giving each group a different set of Bible verses to read (you can combine these if you don't have enough groups for all the verses)—

- Luke 12:40, Luke 17:23-24
- Matthew 24:40-50
- Revelation 6:12-17
- 1 Thessalonians 5:1-3
- Isaiah 13:6-12
- Zephaniah 1:14-18
- Matthew 25:1-13
- Matthew 25:14-30
- Matthew 25:31-46
- 1 Corinthians 15:51-57
- 1 Thessalonians 4:15-18
- Revelation 21:1-8
- Revelation 20:11-15
- Isaiah 34:4, Joel 3:15-16, Zechariah 14:4

All these verses describe the second coming of Christ—some are parables, so you might have to help your kids out. After each group has read their verse, gather as a group and have each group summarize each set of verses. You may want to have some groups read their verses aloud. Make a master list of what the second coming will be like. How do these verses make your kids feel? What do these verses say about the power and authority of Christ? What assurance can Christians have about his return?

THE DISCUSSION, BY NUMBERS

1. You may receive a lot of different answers. Some may foresee technological advances, the future decline of morality, the environment, and other social problems. Make a list of these predictions.

2. Examine the various responses of your kids, asking why they feel the way they do. Why would a non-Christian not want Christ to come back? What about a Christian?

3. Each of these statements has the potential for further discussion and you may want to probe some issues further. Remember that even theologians and Bible teachers can't agree on the specifics of Christ's return. But what do your kids think?

4. Postulate what it might be like if Christ returned today. What regrets might people today have? Why or why not? What would your kids do differently and why?

5. Have the students share their views. Ask if Christ's return really matters to them in terms of the way they plan to live their lives.

THE CLOSE

You may have had a lot of questions and discussion items during this TalkSheet. Summarize the different points made during the discussion. What did your kids learn about the return of Christ? How have their feelings or views of Christ changed? Why or why not? Explain that the return of Christ is uncertain, and may be frightening to some. Those who love Jesus don't have anything to worry about—but they've got to be ready for him to come anytime. Finally, close with this challenge for your group—Jesus told us in his own words that no one will know when he will return (Matthew 24:36), but he will return. Are they ready?

MORE

● You may want to invite the pastor of your church to answer the group's questions regarding Christ's return. Here are some questions to get the discussion going—
⇨ Why is the return of Christ so important?
⇨ What will happen when Christ does return?
⇨ When do you think Christ will return?
⇨ Why didn't Jesus tell us when he was coming back?
⇨ How has the doctrine of the second coming of Christ affected your life?

● If you want to talk more about the second coming of Christ, consider taking this TalkSheet further. Spend some time reading some passages from Revelation and talking about them with your group. This is sometimes a hard chapter to grasp the meaning of—if you choose to do this, make sure that your group is interested in learning more. Check out the *Teen Devotional Bible* (Zondervan) for editor's notes and further explanations. Or use a Bible reference guide, or other Bible reference handbook, to help your kids understand the passages.

LOVE AND FEAR IN THE TIME OF AIDS

1. What is the first thing that comes to mind when you hear the word AIDS?

2. Put an X somewhere on the line below indicating how concerned you are about AIDS.

◆ ▌▌▌▌▌▌▌▌▌▌▌▌▌▌▌▌▌▌▌▌▌ ◆

Very concerned   Not concerned at all

3. Rank the following people with AIDS from those you are **(1) most concerned about** to **(7) least concerned about.**

___ An infant
___ A sexually active, heterosexual teenager
___ A homosexual
___ An intravenous drug user
___ A recipient of a blood transfusion
___ A person living in a third world country
___ An HIV-infected person who consciously spreads the disease

4. What do you think? Would you **A (agree)** or **D (disagree)** with each of these statements?

___ You can recognize someone who is an HIV carrier.
___ Safe sex is the answer to the problem of AIDS.
___ AIDS is God's punishment for homosexuals.
___ AIDS is an easily preventable disease.
___ A cure for AIDS will change people's sexual attitudes and behaviors.
___ Teenagers are at great risk for getting AIDS.
___ AIDS is different than other sexually transmitted diseases.
___ Christians need not worry about AIDS.
___ A person with AIDS is not a child of God.
___ There is a cure for AIDS.

5. How has AIDS made society think differently about sex?

6. Choose one of the following passages from the Bible to rewrite it in your own words.
2 Corinthians 7:1   Colossians 3:2-4   1 Peter 1:13-16

From *More High School TalkSheets—Updated!* by David Lynn. Permission to reproduce this page granted only for use in the buyer's own youth group. www.YouthSpecialties.com

LOVE AND FEAR IN THE TIME OF AIDS [AIDS]

THIS WEEK

What do your kids know about AIDS? What misconceptions have they gotten from their parents, teachers, friends, the media, or the church? Although they've heard about it from school, it's important to discuss AIDS and how it relates to Christianity, their beliefs, and the church at large.

OPENER

Take a sealed envelope and hold it up before the group. Ask how they would feel if you had a list of students in the envelope who tested positive for the AIDS virus—students sitting right there with them. Would they want to know the names? Then explore why they would or would not want to know. Would it make them feel differently about the person? Why or why not? Would it cause them to make unfair judgments about each other if they knew? Would it change the friendships within the group? Change dating relationships?

THE DISCUSSION, BY NUMBERS

1. AIDS, or Acquired Immune Deficiency Syndrome, is a disease that attacks the immune system of the body. Allow the students the opportunity to share their opinions about this deadly disease.

2. How concerned are your kids about AIDS? Why are some more concerned than others? Who should be more concerned—those who are homosexuals or sexually active? How about others? How concerned should Christians be?

3. Ask for volunteers to share their rankings for this question. Why they would or would not be concerned about certain individuals? Point out how Jesus treated those with leprosy—does this relate to those with AIDS? Why or why not?

4. Talk about some of the myths associated with AIDS. The following are facts that kids need to know.
   - You can't get AIDS from casual contact like shaking hands or hugging someone.
   - Safe sex is a myth. The best way to avoid contracting the disease is to abstain from premarital sex. Abstinence for those who are single and monogamy for those who are married to an uninfected partner are the best methods for stopping the sexual spread of the disease.
   - You can't recognize an HIV carrier simply by looking at them.
   - AIDS isn't a punishment from God for sexual sin or for homosexuals.

- People can get AIDS from blood transfusions and other ways, besides having sex.
- For the most part, AIDS is a preventable disease. You may want to spend some time talking about the emphasis placed by society on finding a cure rather than changing immoral lifestyles.
- In general, AIDS is a more devastating and fatal disease than the other STDs.
- Christians should be concerned, because people with the disease—as well as their friends and loved ones—need our compassion and God's love.

5. Explore the changes you and the group have noticed as a result of the AIDS epidemic—and compare these changes to those of the sexual revolution. You may want to briefly explain that the introduction and popularity of birth control pills in the 1950s eliminated one of the biggest deterrents of sexual promiscuity—pregnancy. This paved the way for the sexual revolution of the 60s. Has AIDs paved the way for abstinence?

6. Ask for volunteers to read what they have written. Explore how these passages relate to AIDS.

THE CLOSE

Review the points made during the discussion and point out that those people with AIDS are just like everyone else. AIDS is a disease, just like cancer or any other disease—it's not a curse from God. Christians need to take God's love to people who have AIDS or any other disease. And it's important to realize that AIDS isn't associated just with homosexuality—many heterosexuals and children are living with it or have died of it. Christ died for all people and loves them equally—either with or without AIDS.

MORE

- To help answer questions your kids may have, you can get more information on AIDS from your local Red Cross or public health department. Or check out these Web sites—American Foundation for AIDS Research (www.amfar.org), HIV/AIDS Treatment Information Service (www.hivatis.org), or AIDS Research Information Center (www.critpath.org/aric).
- Want to take this discussion on sexual behavior and attitudes further? Check out *Good Sex: A Whole-Person Approach to Teenage Sexuality and God* (Youth Specialties). For more information, visit www.YouthSpecialties.com.

TALK IT THROUGH

Note: The term parent in the following items refers to all kinds of parenting adults—birth, step, foster, or guardian.

1. On a scale of **1 to 5 (1 being "we hardly ever talk" and 5 being "we talk all the time")**, how often do you talk about each of the following with one or both of your parents or guardians?

   ___ School grades   ___ Family rules   ___ Problems you have

   ___ Internet, TV or movies   ___ Alcohol or drugs   ___ How your day went

   ___ Chores   ___ Your free time   ___ Disobedience

   ___ Christian beliefs   ___ Popular music   ___ Sex

   ___ Clothes and fashion   ___ Church

   ___ Your friends   ___ Your responsibilities

2. When you talk with one or both of your parents, who usually starts it?

   ❑ I usually do.   ❑ My dad usually does.

   ❑ My mom usually does.   ❑ Equal between my dad and me.

   ❑ Equal between my mom and me.   ❑ We never talk.

3. Have you shared your feelings about any of the following with your parents? If so, check those that apply.

   ❑ Family rules   ❑ Chores   ❑ Family relationships

   ❑ Christianity and church   ❑ Friendships   ❑ Sex

   ❑ Your interests   ❑ Your social activities   ❑ Disobedience

   ❑ Your future plans   ❑ Schoolwork   ❑ Your problems

   ❑ Politics   ❑ Fears   ❑ Alcohol or drugs

   ❑ Sibling problems   ❑ Problems in our society   ❑ Your music

   ❑ Feelings

4. If you could change **one thing** about the way you and your parents or guardians talk to each other, what would it be?

5. Each of the following passages relates in some way to communicating. Choose one to read and write in your own words what it says about communication.

   Job 2:13   Proverbs 15:1   James 1:19

   Proverbs 2:3-6   2 Timothy 2:7   James 3:9-12

From *More High School TalkSheets—Updated!* by David Lynn. Permission to reproduce this page granted only for use in the buyer's own youth group. www.YouthSpecialties.com

TALK IT THROUGH [family communication]

THIS WEEK

Communication between parents and teenagers is important, but it often doesn't happen enough. Parents (or guardians) fear they can't talk with their kids like they used to. Kids wonder why their parents need to talk so much. Parents feel like they're running out of time to tell their kids all they will need to know—kids think they know it all. Use this TalkSheet time to examine the vital issue of communication and encourage more parent-teen dialogue.

OPENER

Note: The term parent here and in the following items refers to all kinds of parenting adults—birth, step, foster, or guardian.

For this activity, write some of the following questions (and whatever other ones you want to add) on pieces of paper. Put these slips of paper into a question box for your kids to pull questions from.

- What would say to your parents to get out of being grounded?
- What would you do if one of your parents wants to talk with you about sex?
- Describe the silliest talk you have ever had with a parent.
- How do you get your parents to let you use the car?
- If you could ask your parents any question and they would tell the truth, what question would you ask?
- How do you get money out of your parents when you need it.
- What do you do if your mom or dad asks you about your date last night?
- If you could talk with your parents about anything, and later they'd forget what was said—what would you talk or ask about?

Have your kids take turns drawing the questions and answering them.

THE DISCUSSION, BY NUMBERS

1. On a poster board or a whiteboard, write down which issues your kids talk with their parents about most often. Do the same for those issues that are rarely or never discussed. Ask the group members to summarize what this says about their overall communication with their parents.

2. Talk about who has the responsibility for communication. Do young people have to wait for their parents? What if their parents don't want to talk or aren't very good at communicating?

3. Are there any issues that your kids should be talking over with their parents but aren't? Summarize the group's sharing of personal views into a statement or two.

4. Is there a common theme among your group's responses? Ask the students how they can bring about change by changing their own behaviors.

5. Discuss the verses and summarize on a whiteboard or overhead what they have to say about family communication.

THE CLOSE

You may have gotten a variety of responses from this discussion—some kids get along well with parents but others can't stand them. Point out that communication with parents is important, and your kids can learn a thing or two. Encourage them to trust their parents—and give their parents a fair chance to communicate with them. After all, communication goes two ways (that's why it's called dialog!). What separates them? Why do some kids have better relationships with their parents than others? What can your kids do to hold up their end of the relationship? And point out that the Big Daddy upstairs is listening to them all the time—he's waiting for them to talk with him, too! Close with a time of prayer for your kids and their parents.

MORE

- Hold a talk show with your kids and some of their parents! Your group members will be the audience, and will ask questions or write down their questions in advance. Have the host introduce the guests and the topic of the show. Provide the host with two to three sample questions to start off the show. Here's a few suggestions—what would you like to see teenagers talk with their parents about? How often should parents and their kids sit down and talk? Why aren't parents more understanding of their kids when they talk with them? If you could tell young people only one thing about parents, what would it be?

- Some of your group members might not have good relationships with their parents, or they may know of other kids who don't. Unfortunately, physical and sexual abuse happens within churched families too. Encourage your kids to talk with a trusted adult—including you, if they want. For more information on dealing with abuse, check out the National Exchange Club Foundation (www.preventchildabuse.com) or the American Humane Association (www.americanhumane.org), Rape, Abuse, and Incest National Network (www.rainn.org), The Family Violence Prevention Fund (www.fvpf.org), or Christians In Recovery (www.christians-in-recovery.com).

KILLER TUNES

1. If you could interview a music group whose lyrics promoted violence and vulgarity, what would be the most important question you would ask?

2. What do you think? Read the statements and decide if you **A (agree)**, **D (disagree)**, or **U (unsure)**.

___ Violent music lyrics provide positive solutions to societal problems.

___ To its fans, violent music is a religion.

___ Violent and vulgar music is merely entertainment.

___ Teenagers don't just listen to violent music lyrics—they live violent music lyrics.

___ Violent music exploits teenagers.

___ Violent music lyrics desensitize the listener to moral purity.

___ Violent music concerts should be more closely regulated by authorities.

___ There's something different about teenagers who enjoy violent music lyrics.

___ Violent music is the music of the world.

___ Christian music that sounds like the violent music of today encourages kids to listen to violent music.

3. Check which of the following problems you think violent music contributes to.

❑ Rebellion
❑ Suicide
❑ Family conflict
❑ Alcohol or drug use
❑ Satanism
❑ Vandalism
❑ Pornography
❑ Permissive sexual attitudes

❑ Alienation
❑ Destructive behavior
❑ Exploitative sex
❑ Profanity
❑ Agnosticism
❑ Psychological problems
❑ Racism
❑ Apathy

❑ Violence
❑ Sexual stereotyping
❑ Aggression
❑ Hatred and anger
❑ School difficulties
❑ Spiritual decline
❑ Depression
❑ Risky behavior

4. Which items are true for you?

❑ I agree with the ideas stated in violent music lyrics.

❑ I agree with the lifestyle choices of music band members.

❑ I agree with the way these band members dress.

❑ I agree with what occurs at the concerts of bands who promote violence.

❑ I agree with the visual images portrayed in these kinds of music videos, posters, Web sites, and tee shirts.

5. Check out Colossians 2:8, How does this verse apply to violent music?

KILLER TUNES [violent music]

THIS WEEK

Teens today are exposed to more violent music than before—much of it pushed by harder and more violent themes. The angry lyrics come in various kinds—gangster rap, alternative, hard core, grunge, punk, and so on. This TalkSheet offers the opportunity to discuss these forms of violent music, which are having a profound influence on young people.

OPENER

You may want to arrange to have a music CD that has violent, angry lyrics playing as group members arrive. (Choose carefully!) Observe their reactions. Were they annoyed, excited, or ignoring the music? Then point out the reactions to the group. How did the music make them feel? Were they surprised to hear the music here? Why or why not?

Ask your kids to name a number of bands that promote violence with their lyrics. Make a list of these groups. Which ones are popular with kids at their school? What do their lyrics promote—drugs, alcohol, sex, abuse, rape? How do your kids think this music influences people? Do they notice a difference in the kids at school who listen to this music and those who don't? What are the differences? Do they act differently, more violently? Why or why not?

THE DISCUSSION, BY NUMBERS

1. How did your kids respond? What would they ask and why? How would they expect these questions to be answered?

2. Take time to explore each of these statements. You may want to explain to your students how violent music can become a religion for some kids, with the lyrics becoming a theology of hate, violence, and exploitative sex. What are the consequences of teenagers living out violent music lyrics as a philosophy of life?

3. What items did your kids pick and why? You may want to make a master list of these and talk about how music influences people and society.

4. Where did your kids stand on these? Let your kids talk about these and debate them if they disagree.

5. Create a large list of all of the deceptive philosophies being promoted by violent music lyrics that the group identified. How is violent music one of Satan's tools?

THE CLOSE

Wrap up this discussion by giving your kids something to think about, but avoid bashing the bands and musicians that they bring up during the discussion—some of your kids do listen to this music and like it. Give them the freedom to reach their own conclusions about individual violent music performers and keep your comments general. One of the strongest impacts you can have on your group is to simply summarize the points made during the discussion. Reflecting on what has been said by the kids themselves about violent music will be much more powerful than any sermonizing on your part.

You may want to close on a positive note by pointing out to your group members that they don't have to accept the values imposed by this style of music. They can continue to learn more about Christ and his kingdom using the Bible as a framework for living, rather than the values taught by violent and sexually explicit music.

MORE

● You may want to have your kids bring in their favorite CDs. Or find a music magazine or catalog (like BMG or Columbia House) to look at with your group. Pick out some different artists and styles of music. Or pick some titles from the Web sites listed below. Possibly read the description of the CD or some lyrics from inside. With your group, create a standard for rating the CDs like movies are rated (G, PG, PG-13, R, NC-17). Be sure to include everyone's input and ideas. Then rate the CDs and discuss the reasons why each was given the rating it received.

● If you want to take this discussion further, talk about the influences of violent music on people. Focus on satanic music and the influences of music that promote rape, sexual abuse, physical abuse, drug abuse, alcohol abuse, hatred, and more. How will listeners act when saturated with these messages? Point out that what people fill their heads with will come out ("garbage in, garbage out"). How does this music influence kids to swear more, become more violent, or change their relationships with others? For more information on music and reviews (both Christian and non) of all kinds of music, check out Plugged In Magazine (www.family.org/pplace/pi), Billboard (www.billboard-online.com/reviews), CD Shakedown (www.cdshakedown.com), MTV (www.mtv.com), or Wall of Sound (http://wallof-sound.go.com/reviews).

THE JOY FACTOR

1. How content or happy are you today? Check one—
   - ❏ Very content and happy
   - ❏ Kind of content and happy
   - ❏ Neutral
   - ❏ Kind of discontented and unhappy
   - ❏ Very discontented and unhappy

2. Put an arrow by the phrases that describe happiness to you.

   A purpose in life   Good grades   Success
   Salvation   Health   Great friends
   Good looks   A positive family life   Being young
   Service to others   Sex   Spending private time with
   A good job   Being loved   God
   New clothes   A boyfriend or girlfriend
   Material things   Popularity

3. Read the statement and decide if you **A (agree)** or **D (disagree)**.
   ___ Happiness and contentment are important goals in life.
   ___ Happiness and contentment are moods.
   ___ Happiness and contentment are easier for people with a lot of money.
   ___ Happiness and contentment can lead to selfishness they're your main concern.
   ___ Happiness and contentment aren't something everyone can have.
   ___ The happiness and contentment of teenagers is the responsibility of their parents.

4. Check your answer to each of the following questions.

	None of the time	Half of the time	All of the time
How often do you feel sad?	❏	❏	❏
How often do you feel lonely?	❏	❏	❏
How often do you feel afraid?	❏	❏	❏
How often do you feel stressed?	❏	❏	❏
How often do you feel far away from God?	❏	❏	❏
How often do you feel down?	❏	❏	❏

5. Is this true for you or not?
   I feel satisfied with the direction my life is going.

6. Read **Matthew 5:1-12**. Why are the people Christ described happy or blessed?

From *More High School TalkSheets—Updated!* by David Lynn. Permission to reproduce this page granted only for use in the buyer's own youth group. www.YouthSpecialties.com

THE JOY FACTOR [happiness]

THIS WEEK

More than any other age group, young people indicate their desire to be happy—but do they know what they want? What brings them happiness and why? This TalkSheet discusses happiness versus joy and Christianity versus the world's understanding of happiness.

Be sensitive to your group members during this discussion. Some of your kids aren't happy at all—they may be dealing with issues such as divorce, abuse, depression, failing grades, break ups, and more.

OPENER

Ask your kids how their perceptions of happiness have changed over the years. What used to make your kids happy when they were little? What about now? How will their perception of happiness change over the years? How does growing up alter happiness or change its meaning?

Or for something different, you may want to pass out newspapers or magazines and have the students find as many examples of happiness as they can in three minutes. What do the advertisements say about happiness? Why does society base their happiness on material possessions and money?

THE DISCUSSION, BY NUMBERS

1. Give the group the chance to share their feelings and give an explanation why. How often do they or others fake happiness? Point out how happiness is often circumstantial.

2. Put the list on the whiteboard or poster board and then ask the group to identify the top five or so items that people their age would say bring happiness. Now ask the group to share those they checked. Was there a difference between the average kid and your kids? Why or why not? Is there a difference between those who are and aren't Christians? Which of the things on the list are worth building one's life around?

3. The young people will likely think of additional things, so create a master list on a whiteboard or on newsprint. What items did your group members check and why?

4. Get an overall picture by asking the kids if they see a correlation or relationship between each of the questions. For example, did the people who felt sad also report feeling far away from God? Challenge your kids to look for patterns in their lives. Are there certain times when they feel down? All the time?

5. Ask the young people to explain their answers. Should the direction they are going stay the same or should it change? If it needs to change, are they willing to make the necessary changes?

6. Carefully study the list of happy or blessed people Christ described. Does the list have much in common with what we normally consider happiness to be? It seems Jesus described happiness as something totally foreign to most. Why is God's kingdom different than the world?

THE CLOSE

Happiness and contentment are conditional, but joy—given by God's Spirit—brings happiness even in times of doubt, pain, worry, and struggle. And while some people think of happiness as outward because of things or circumstances, that's just not God's way. The Bible says that happiness is an attitude that comes from being content. Paul, writing to the Philippians, said he had learned to be content with plenty or with little. He could live through either circumstance through the strength given by Christ (Philippians 4:11-13). Paul had learned to rise above his circumstances because he knew that they couldn't provide happiness. The Bible calls this joy.

What do your kids need to do to find God's joy? Pray more? Get closer to him? Get right with their friends or parents? Encourage your kids to find what is making them discontent and to fix it, with God's help.

MORE

● You may want to take some time to look more in depth at Paul's life. What a life this guy had! He was converted by becoming blind, had a "thorn in the flesh," endured a shipwreck, numerous floggings, and more. Read some chapters on Paul's life in Acts and discuss them with your group. How did Paul handle these situations? How can these be an example for our lives today? What does Paul's life say about God's faithfulness and love?

● Do you sense that there are larger issues within your group that is causing unhappiness? Are there kids dealing with the pain of divorce, depression, guilt, and more? Spend some time talking about these with your group and encourage them to pray about these. Encourage them to find someone to talk to—including you—who they feel comfortable with. For more information and links, see these TalkSheets—Got Faith? (page 109), Hooked on Drugs (page 61), Too Much Too Soon (page 69), "My Parents Split Up" (page 65), and Down and Out (page 73).

NO PLACE TO CALL HOME

1. What is your most common reaction to **homelessness**?
When I see a homeless person on the street, I feel—

- ❏ Afraid
- ❏ Indifferent
- ❏ Angry
- ❏ Sympathetic

- ❏ Disgusted
- ❏ Annoyed
- ❏ Strange
- ❏ Helpless

- ❏ Confused
- ❏ Offended
- ❏ Content
- ❏ Superior

2. Who are **most homeless** people? Check your top three answers.

- ❏ Mentally ill people
- ❏ Criminals
- ❏ Elderly people
- ❏ Poor people
- ❏ Minorities

- ❏ Families
- ❏ Alcoholics
- ❏ Runaway teens
- ❏ Lazy bums
- ❏ Unemployed people

- ❏ Physically disabled people
- ❏ Drug addicts
- ❏ Single-parent families

3. What do you think these statements—do you **A (agree)** or **D (disagree)**?

___ Most Christians don't care to help the homeless.
___ The homeless have serious disabilities that keep them homeless.
___ Homeless people don't want to help themselves.
___ Homelessness exists because of a lack of housing.
___ There's nothing that can be done to help the homeless.
___ If Christians don't help the homeless, no one will.
___ Homelessness is the government's problem.
___ The homeless must learn to fend for themselves.
___ Churches could do more to help the homeless.

4. On the scale below, indicate to what degree you are **different** from or **similar to** homeless people.

◆ ▌▌▌▌▌▌▌▌▌▌▌▌▌▌▌▌▌▌▌▌▌ ◆

Very similar   Not the same at all

5. Check out Matthew 25:37-45 and briefly describe how your youth group could provide at least two of the following for the homeless.

Food	Spiritual healing	Church services	Special services
Healthcare	Job training	Clothing	Shelter

From *More High School TalkSheets—Updated!* by David Lynn. Permission to reproduce this page granted only for use in the buyer's own youth group. www.YouthSpecialties.com

NO PLACE TO CALL HOME [homeless people]

THIS WEEK

High schoolers are well aware of the problem of homelessness. They see people aimlessly walking the streets, the "will work for food" signs, and reports of the problem on the news. Homelessness is a visible problem in the United States and other parts of the world. But even though the problem is readily recognized, it's quite misunderstood. Use this TalkSheet to help clear up some of the misconceptions about the issue and to challenge your students to become part of the solution in the name of Jesus.

OPENER

You may want to have someone unknown to the group impersonate a homeless person. This person should play and dress the part—and be able to address the issues of homelessness and answer difficult questions your kids might have. Some of these may include why they can't get a job or what made them homeless.

For a different twist, you could also ask the manager or someone from a homeless shelter to come in and talk about the problem with the group. Because they have firsthand experience, they may be able to share stories about and discuss the problems of a homeless family—food, shelter, medical care, spiritual problems, life-threatening problems, and so on.

THE DISCUSSION, BY NUMBERS

1. Create a list of the feelings shared by students. You probably will be able to generate a larger list than the one found in the activity. Ask the students why they feel the way they do. Investigate what kind of experiences students have had with the homeless—caricatures viewed on television, past work with the homeless, and so on.

2. Use this activity to identify the different stereotypes people have of the homeless, from the victim down on his luck to the tramp who prefers the lifestyle of the transient. Also talk about what a home provides for people—shelter, protection, dignity, security, and status.

3. Poll the kids on their answers to these statements. If everyone agreed on a particular one, go on to the next. If there is a wide difference of opinion, discuss the pros and cons.

4. How are your kids and the homeless alike? Where did they rate themselves on this scale? Take some time to talk about how different or similar they are to those who are homeless. What do they have in common besides physical belongings?

Point out to your kids that homeless people are created in the image of God, just like them.

5. Ask the group how serious Christ was when he delivered this parable. If Christ was serious, how serious will we be in acting on his words?

THE CLOSE

Review the different points made during the discussion. Point out that the problem of homelessness arises from a multitude of conditions existing in our society. There are homeless because of alcoholism, drug addiction, unemployment, chronic mental illness, physical disabilities, AIDS, domestic violence, single-parent families, and government policies on affordable housing—just to name the major contributing factors. Some of these people don't want help. They prefer their chosen lifestyles. But most of the homeless want help desperately. Government assistance and homeless shelters have not been able to eliminate the problem.

Emphasize that many homeless people need much more than just shelter. Christ waits for his people to touch the lives of the homeless in his name. Remind the group that Christ was homeless also (Matthew 8:20; Luke 9:58).

MORE

● Role-play the homeless situation with your kids—give each of them a specific problem, such as losing their job, getting divorced, being a single parent, suffering from AIDS, being abused at home, being hooked on cocaine, or being forced into prostitution. Or would they answer those who asked them questions like "What is wrong with you?" How would these situations affect their lives? You may want to have other kids question them and see what it's like for the homeless person to explain where they are and why.

● Or you and a few of your kids may want to dress the part and sit on a corner asking for food or money (be sure to get other adults to help you out and keep an eye on your kids) How do other people react to them? What looks do they get and how to they feel? Did holding a homeless sign or "will work for food" help them? Debrief with the group and talk about experiencing homelessness from the other side.

WAGING WAR

1. Do you know someone who has fought in a war? Which one?

2. Rank the following social problems from your **biggest concern (1)** to your **smallest concern (10)**.

___ Crime   ___ Child abuse
___ Hunger   ___ Discrimination
___ Poverty   ___ Sexual abuse and rape
___ Alcohol or drug abuse   ___ Family breakdown
___ War or the threat of war   ___ Environment

3. What do you think? Do you **A (agree)** or **D (disagree)**?

___ Some video games promote war.
___ War is exciting.
___ There's nothing good about war.
___ It's patriotic to support war.
___ War is avoidable.
___ People should have the right to protest against a war.
___ War is never right.
___ My generation will fight in a war.
___ War promotes peace.
___ Resisting a military draft is a sin.
___ Small children should be discouraged from playing with war-type toys.
___ Young people should be willing to die for their country.

4. If your country were to go to war, what would you do?

❑ Never fight, no matter what the reason for the war.
❑ Fight, but only if I thought the war was justified.
❑ Fight, whether or not I thought the war was right.

5. Pick one of the following passages from the Bible to rewrite in your own words.
Proverbs 12:20
Matthew 5:9
James 3:17, 18

From *More High School TalkSheets—Updated!* by David Lynn. Permission to reproduce this page granted only for use in the buyer's own youth group. www.YouthSpecialties.com

WAGING WAR [war]

THIS WEEK

Teenagers play war-related video games, watch war movies, and see news coverage of wars around the world. They generally have a distorted and glorified picture of war. This TalkSheet gives your kids the chance to examine a realistic, biblical view of war An additional TalkSheet covering the topic of nuclear war can be found on page 49.

If you or your church takes a strong position on either side of the war and peace issue, you may use this discussion as a way to help your kids understand your view as well as to form one of their own.

OPENER

For a fun and fast-paced opener, break your kids into small groups. Give each group a piece of paper and something to write with. Then give each group one minute to write down as many war movie titles as possible. For each correct war movie title, each team gets a point. The team with the most correct titles and points gets a prize (of your choice). Compare these titles and ask the kids what each movie is about. How does each portray war? What was the theme of the movie? Do they remember which war the movie was about? Do your kids think these movies accurately portray war?

For an extensive list of all war movie titles, check out The Internet Movie Database at http://us.imdb.com/.

THE DISCUSSION, BY NUMBERS

1. How many people do your kids know who have been in a war? What stories have they heard? What impression about war have they gotten from these people? Allow time for the students to share stories of individuals they may know who have been wounded or killed as a result of war.

2. What social problems are the worst? Are these problems worth fighting in war for? Make a list and rank them as a group. Is there currently a war going on because of any of these issues?

3. Read the statements aloud and ask for some kids to express their opinions. Ask the students to explain their answers—not everyone will agree, but all should be allowed to air their opinions.

4. This personalizes the war issue in a way that forces kids to consider their beliefs about war. Offer different potential war scenarios and see how students respond.

5. Divide the teens into small groups and have each interpret one of these verses regarding war and peace. Ask the groups how consistent the verses

are with the way their government creates and maintains policy. What can they do to be peacemakers?

THE CLOSE

War is sometimes inevitable to keep world peace and protect the countries of the world. War is the price people pay for freedom and justice. Christians, in particular, should fight for and promote peace, acceptance, and love.

Don't leave this discussion in a negative light. God is still on the throne and in control of what happens in today's world. Christians can find hope in Christ as they spread his love—and they can begin right here where they live—on the school bus or in the cafeteria. Emphasize that each of them can be a peacemaker.

Conclude the discussion by examining James 4:1-3 and a time of prayer for world peace and situations of war that may be going on.

MORE

● Some of your kids may not have an accurate picture of what war is. You may want to ask someone that you know—possibly a member of your church—who has been involved in war to come in and talk to your group. Encourage your kids to ask questions about what is involved in war and the tragedies that occur.

● One cause of war is the persecution of certain ethnic or religious groups and conflict among members of one country. You may want to try a role-play game called Romans and Christians (going way back to the days after Christ, when the Christians were intensely persecuted...and killed). Split your group up into two groups—one of Romans and the other as Christians. It works best to play this game at night in a field, large building, or wooded area. Plant a light (a torch, candle, or fire) somewhere unknown to both groups and give each of the Romans a flashlight. The goal of the Christians is to get to the light—and the Romans want to stop them. The Romans must hunt the Christians down and if they find one, they must put them in a jail. And only way for the Christians to get out of jail is to try to "convert" the Roman jail guard by quoting Bible passages, telling a story about Christ, or singing a song. The game ends when all the Christians have made it to the light (or if you've played for a long time!).

Debrief the game and talk about how each group felt. What was scary about being hunted down? For more information on persecution within the church, check out *Student Underground* (Youth Specialties).

FAMILY MATTERS

1. Describe one of your favorite times you spent with your family.

2. Do you **agree** with this statement?

   No one will influence you more than your family.

   Why do you think this?

3. What do you think? Read the statements and answer **Y (yes)** or **N (no)**.
   ___ Our society is more concerned about the individual than the family.
   ___ Family life is as good as it has ever been.
   ___ Teenagers should have no obligations to their families.
   ___ Families experience more problems today than in the past.
   ___ Families should ask for outside help when they are having problems.

4. Check the following statement that best describes how you feel.
   ❏ There's a good reason why my family is together as a family.
   ❏ There are times when I wonder why my family is together as a family.
   ❏ There's absolutely no reason for my family to be together as a family.

5. Think through the following questions and answer them below.
   How are you getting as much from your family life as you can?

   How are you giving as much to your family life as you can?

6. Decide from reading these verses which of the following families is closest to yours.
   1 Samuel 2:12
   1 Kings 15:1-3
   2 Kings 15:1-4
   Luke 15:11-16
   2 Timothy 1:5

From *More High School TalkSheets—Updated!* by David Lynn. Permission to reproduce this page granted only for use in the buyer's own youth group. www.YouthSpecialties.com

FAMILY MATTERS [family life]

THIS WEEK

The structure of the family has undergone enormous changes in recent years. Today there are different types of families within society—traditional families, divorced families, single-parent families, or foster families. This TalkSheet will let you talk with your kids about their families and the role of family in their lives.

Pay close attention to your group during this discussion. Don't assume that all your kids live in a traditional two-parent home! Be extra sensitive to those kids who may be feeling the hurt and confusion of divorce and family separation.

OPENER

The word *family* is used several times throughout the Bible to describe human families, the spiritual family, and as an analogy for the family in heaven. You may want to start by having small groups of your kids find verses that talk about a family or deal with a family. Nearly every biblical character in the Old Testament came from a family. Take some time to study a few of these Bible characters and families (and others that your group finds)—Noah, Abraham, Isaac, Jacob, David, Ruth, Samson, and so on. What was unique about each of these family situations? What struggles or problems did the families have? How does this relate to family problems today? What does God teach about the family in the Bible? What other thoughts on families does your group have from reading these verses?

THE DISCUSSION, BY NUMBERS

1. When asking your young people to share their memories, be sensitive to families who are split or divorced, but keep in mind that these families still share good times, too.

2. Do your kids agree? Why or why not? Some kids won't like to admit that their families have influenced them at all. Others are worried about the negative influence their dysfunctional families have had on them. Ask the young people to identify how their families have influenced them, positively and negatively.

3. Have the students share their thoughts and debate the issues that come out of this discussion. What responsibilities will your kids have to their families as they grow older and establish their own particular identities?

4. This activity focuses your young people on the mission of their families. If they don't feel they are getting what they need out of their families, where will they turn? Explain that some kids turn to gang involvement, others to a dysfunctional peer group or an unhealthy male or female relationship. In addition to their families, where else can young people get the love and support they need?

5. This continues where question 4 left off. Ask the young people to share how they are getting and giving what they need from their families.

6. Each of these passages describes various levels of family devotion to God. How can your kids involve God in their families? How about in their future families?

THE CLOSE

Close by positively affirming the need for family, but be sensitive to those kids in your group with broken families. Point out that every family is different, because each person is different. But no matter what your kids' situations are, you can play a vital role in supporting family life by what you say. You may want to form a circle and pray for each other's families. And encourage any of them who may want to talk about their families with you to do so. Some of your kids might need some individual encouragement and insight. Encourage them to find an adult who they are comfortable with to talk to.

MORE

● You may want to challenge your kids to ask questions of some of their family members. They may find out stuff about their family that they never know before! Below are some questions to use as a guide.

⇨ Who were you named after?
⇨ Did you have a nickname?
⇨ What games did you play growing up?
⇨ What did your father do for his career?
⇨ Did your mother work?
⇨ What was your dad like?
⇨ What did your grandmother look like?

● You may want to talk about family situations that aren't healthy. Some of your kids may be in—or have friends who are in—unhealthy, abusive family situations. If you sense this among your group members, consider talking about this with your group. For more information, check out the National Exchange Club Foundation (www.preventchildabuse.com), or the American Humane Association (www.americanhumane.org), the Rape, Abuse, and Incest National Network (www.rainn.org), The Family Violence Prevention Fund (www.fvpf.org), or Christians In Recovery (www.christians-in-recovery.com).

WHO'S NUMBER ONE?

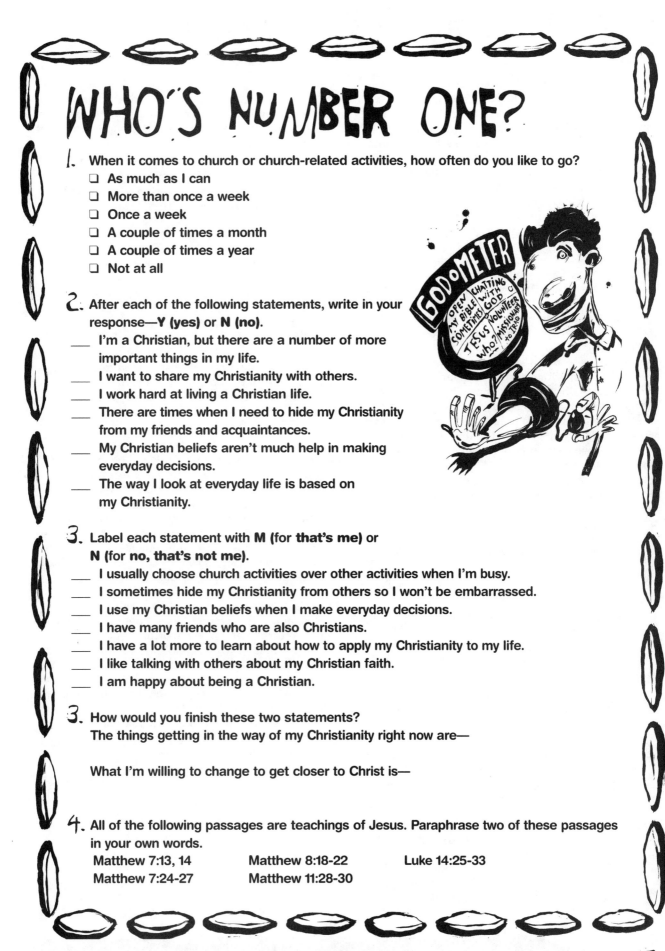

1. When it comes to church or church-related activities, how often do you like to go?
   - ❏ As much as I can
   - ❏ More than once a week
   - ❏ Once a week
   - ❏ A couple of times a month
   - ❏ A couple of times a year
   - ❏ Not at all

2. After each of the following statements, write in your response—**Y (yes)** or **N (no)**.
   ___ I'm a Christian, but there are a number of more important things in my life.
   ___ I want to share my Christianity with others.
   ___ I work hard at living a Christian life.
   ___ There are times when I need to hide my Christianity from my friends and acquaintances.
   ___ My Christian beliefs aren't much help in making everyday decisions.
   ___ The way I look at everyday life is based on my Christianity.

3. Label each statement with **M (for that's me)** or **N (for no, that's not me)**.
   ___ I usually choose church activities over other activities when I'm busy.
   ___ I sometimes hide my Christianity from others so I won't be embarrassed.
   ___ I use my Christian beliefs when I make everyday decisions.
   ___ I have many friends who are also Christians.
   ___ I have a lot more to learn about how to apply my Christianity to my life.
   ___ I like talking with others about my Christian faith.
   ___ I am happy about being a Christian.

3. How would you finish these two statements?
   The things getting in the way of my Christianity right now are—

   What I'm willing to change to get closer to Christ is—

4. All of the following passages are teachings of Jesus. Paraphrase two of these passages in your own words.
   Matthew 7:13, 14   Matthew 8:18-22   Luke 14:25-33
   Matthew 7:24-27   Matthew 11:28-30

From *More High School TalkSheets—Updated!* by David Lynn. Permission to reproduce this page granted only for use in the buyer's own youth group. www.YouthSpecialties.com

WHO'S NUMBER ONE? [putting Christ first]

THIS WEEK

Christian teenagers, if they haven't already done so, are about to come to a fork in the spiritual road. When they were younger they attended church, prayed, and memorized Bible verses because that was what they were supposed to do. But now they have a choice. What importance will Christianity take during their adolescence? Use this TalkSheet as an opportunity to talk about the role of Christianity in the lives of your young people.

OPENER

On a white board or poster board, make a list of what your kids think are important. What would an average person consider to be important? Ideas may include food, family, money, health, and friends. Write all these suggestions down. Where does Christ fit into this list? How long did it take your kids before they mentioned Jesus or God? Now ask the group what a non-Christian would consider to be the most important? A celebrity? A government leader? How about a Christian? Point out that people have different priorities and things that are most important to them, based on their beliefs. Where do your kids' beliefs stand? Is Christ first on their list?

Now have them rate these on a scale. What are the most important things in life? Why do some people think some are more important than others? How will your kids' priorities of importance change as they grow up? Go to college? Get married? Raise a family? Point out that through all this, God never changes. He always stays the same—and is always there, ready for an important place in their lives.

THE DISCUSSION, BY NUMBERS

1. Is church involvement an indicator of how important someone's Christianity is to them? How important is church activity to your group? Why or why not? What does church involvement strengthen one's faith?

2. How did your kids answer this? What answers indicate a higher or lower commitment to Christ? Why or why not?

3. How do your kids handle their faith? Are they surrounded by others who are Christians? How did your kids answer these statements? Take some time to talk about these with your group.

4. No Christian is perfect—all have obstacles standing in the way of a close relationships with Christ. What's in the way of your kids' relationships with him? You may want to ask those who are willing to publicly make a commitment, but don't pressure any of your young people to share.

5. It will be helpful to break the kids into groups to do this activity. Then have the groups come back together and have each group share what they learned.

THE CLOSE

You may want to use the following questions to wrap up the session—How committed do you want to be to your Christian faith? What kind of relationship do you want to have with Jesus Christ? How many things are more important than God?

When God gave the Ten Commandments, he knew that there would be many things that would compete for our attention. This probably explains why the first commandment was first (Exodus 20:3)! Ask your kids this question—what crowds out God in your life? Whatever it is, it is their god. They are committed to something! Ask the students how much of their commitment is directed toward their Christian faith. How can they get closer to God?

You may want to close with time for prayer, giving your group time with God in silent prayer.

MORE

● How important are their Christian beliefs to your group members? Would they like to set goals for themselves—to get closer to God? To put him first? To spend more time with him and less time in front of the TV? It's important for everyone to have spiritual goals. Encourage each group member to write a letter to themselves—stating their spiritual goals and how they want to grow as closer to God. Give them envelopes, which they will address to themselves and seal. Mail the letters to them anywhere from six months to a year.

● Challenge your group to investigate five Bible characters to see how important their faith in God was to them. They will find that, for the most part, the Bible is a book of failures, not successes. This can be a source of encouragement for your young people, since there isn't much difference in people today than in biblical times. You may want to talk about this as a group and point out that God never changes, no matter how badly one messes up. He's always there with open arms.

INTO ALL THE WORLD

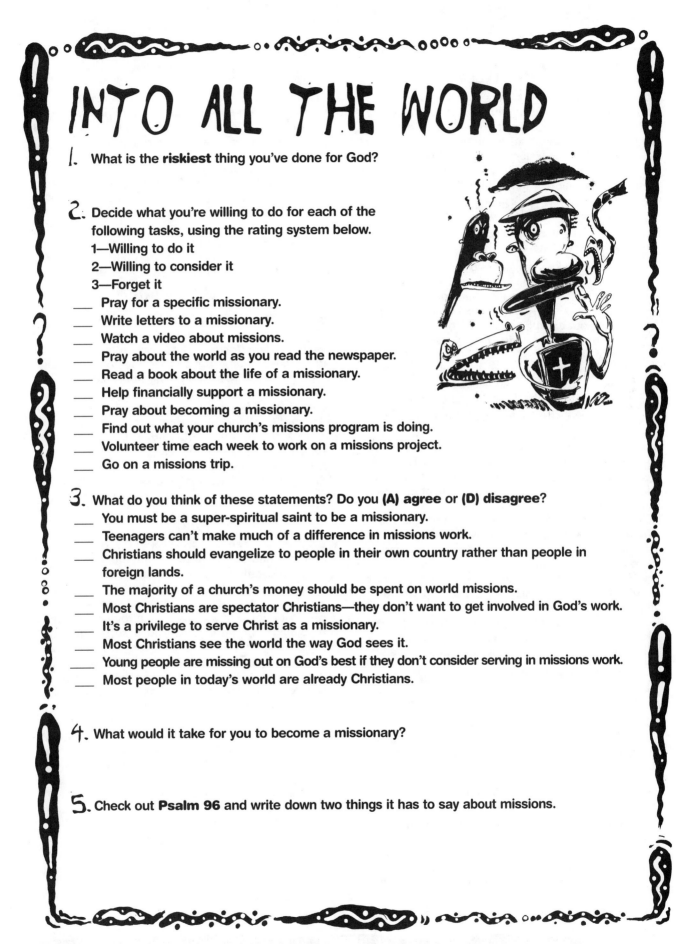

1. What is the **riskiest** thing you've done for God?

2. Decide what you're willing to do for each of the following tasks, using the rating system below.
   1—Willing to do it
   2—Willing to consider it
   3—Forget it
   ___ Pray for a specific missionary.
   ___ Write letters to a missionary.
   ___ Watch a video about missions.
   ___ Pray about the world as you read the newspaper.
   ___ Read a book about the life of a missionary.
   ___ Help financially support a missionary.
   ___ Pray about becoming a missionary.
   ___ Find out what your church's missions program is doing.
   ___ Volunteer time each week to work on a missions project.
   ___ Go on a missions trip.

3. What do you think of these statements? Do you **(A) agree** or **(D) disagree**?
   ___ You must be a super-spiritual saint to be a missionary.
   ___ Teenagers can't make much of a difference in missions work.
   ___ Christians should evangelize to people in their own country rather than people in foreign lands.
   ___ The majority of a church's money should be spent on world missions.
   ___ Most Christians are spectator Christians—they don't want to get involved in God's work.
   ___ It's a privilege to serve Christ as a missionary.
   ___ Most Christians see the world the way God sees it.
   ___ Young people are missing out on God's best if they don't consider serving in missions work.
   ___ Most people in today's world are already Christians.

4. What would it take for you to become a missionary?

5. Check out **Psalm 96** and write down two things it has to say about missions.

From *More High School TalkSheets—Updated!* by David Lynn. Permission to reproduce this page granted only for use in the buyer's own youth group. www.YouthSpecialties.com

INTO ALL THE WORLD [foreign missions]

THIS WEEK

The youth in your church may hear exciting adventure stories about missionaries, see pictures or videos, and pray for missionaries—but do they picture themselves being missionaries? This TalkSheet will open up a discussion on foreign missions and help them understand their part in taking the life-changing message of Jesus Christ to all the world.

OPENER

You may want to start this discussion by asking your group a few questions—

- What do your kids think missionaries are? Christians living in the jungle—learning obscure languages? Those spreading the gospel to the starving people in Africa? People in the inner city reaching out to drug addicts and prostitutes?
- What do missionaries do—besides telling the news of Jesus Christ?
- Who pays missionaries? Where do they get their money, clothes, and other necessities?
- In what regions of the world are there missionaries? What would be the most dangerous place to be?

Your kids may have many different ideas of missions work, based on what they've seen or heard in church or experienced in their own lives. Before this session you may want to find information on several different ministries. There are hundreds of ministries that reach out to people of all ages in nearly all regions of the world. For links to these organizations, check out www.gospelcom.net and browse under the category missions. Point out some of these organizations to your group, including what these missionaries do, where, for what ages, and for what purpose. Also, point out that some missionaries are supported by churches and may not have information on the Internet. Be sure to get some information on the missionaries that your church supports. Where are these missionaries and how long have they been there?

THE DISCUSSION, BY NUMBERS

1. Create a master list of risks, and find out what motivated students to take risks for God. You might want to ask for examples of risk-taking for God from the lives of biblical characters. Explore how afraid the group is of the concept of missions.

2. What's the commitment level of each of the tasks? You may want to wait until you wrap up the discussion before calling the group to commit to any specific tasks.

3. Did your kids agree or disagree? Consider each of the statements and how they apply to winning the world for Christ.

4. Challenge the group with the notion that all Christians are called to be missionaries. What would it take for them to reach out? Where would they want to go or what would they want to do?

5. Examine the passage to see how many truths can be found about missions. For example, (1) verse two says to talk about God's gift of salvation all day long; (2) verse three says to tell all the world about him; (3) verse five says that most people do not know God; (4) verse nine says that all the earth should worship God; and (5) in verse 13 we are told that God is coming to judge the earth.

THE CLOSE

Explain to the group that God has a different plan for the world than his creatures do. Remind your kids that they're focused right now on friends, fun, getting independent. But all that might include doing missionary work. Are they willing to consider it? You may want to read the Great Commission found in Matthew 28:18-20—God has called everyone to reach out! Challenge your kids to think about they can work as agent for Christ today, in their own lives, and in the future. And encourage them to pray for the missionaries worldwide. You may want to close by talking about what you can do as a group to reach out and plan a missions project or reach out.

MORE

- Bring a newspaper to the group. Go through it and examine different local, national, and international events from God's point of view. Ask the group to decide how the gospel could make a difference in each situation you study. Are your kids willing to help out somewhere in the community? If so, consider getting involved with your group!
- Consider hosting a fundraiser for the missionaries in your church, such as a special dinner, dessert night, clothing drive, or other event. Get your kids involved in the planning—and be sure to let the congregation know the purpose of the fundraiser! You may want to check with your church missions committee to see if there is anything in particular that certain missionaries need, such as books, clothing, school supplies, and Bibles. Possibly use the money raised to buy materials for these missionaries.

NUKE 'EM

1. What do you think is the likelihood that nuclear weapons will be used in your lifetime?
   - ❑ It will probably happen
   - ❑ It's somewhat likely
   - ❑ It probably won't happen
   - ❑ Nope, not going to happen

2. What do you think might happen if nuclear weapons are used in the future?

3. Pretend for a moment that you are the newly elected president of a certain country. As president, you have a difficult decision to make. Your country is at war with another nation. Should you—
   - ❑ Use nuclear weapons to end the war sooner and save the lives of your people? or
   - ❑ Continue to use conventional weapons, even though you know more of your people will have to die?

4. Do you **A (agree)** or **D (disagree)** with the statements below?
   - ___ The world powers need more nuclear weapons to maintain world peace.
   - ___ Nuclear weapons could be used on a limited scale without getting out of hand.
   - ___ Only the military has to worry about nuclear weapons and warfare.
   - ___ The average person doesn't know enough about the threat of nuclear war.
   - ___ Countries need nuclear weapons for their self-defense.
   - ___ The threat of nuclear war is one of the biggest problems faced by today's world.
   - ___ The Bible has nothing to say about nuclear war.
   - ___ The next global war will include the use of nuclear weapons.
   - ___ Nuclear war can be prevented.
   - ___ The church should speak out against the threat of nuclear war.
   - ___ Nuclear war really isn't that big of a deal.
   - ___ The world is a safer place to live because of nuclear weapons.

5. Which of these true for you (if any)? Have you ever—
   - ❑ worried about a nuclear war happening in your lifetime?
   - ❑ thought about what it would be like if you survived a nuclear war?
   - ❑ considered how nuclear weapons could affect your children?
   - ❑ wondered what God thinks about nuclear weapons?

6. How do each of these verses apply to nuclear war?
   Romans 12:17-21   1 Peter 3:8-12   James 4:1, 2

From *More High School TalkSheets—Updated!* by David Lynn. Permission to reproduce this page granted only for use in the buyer's own youth group. www.YouthSpecialties.com

NUKE 'EM [nuclear war]

THIS WEEK

As long as nuclear weapons exist, their use is a possibility. Anytime there is a world crisis, the threat is there. Study after study has examined the fear, uncertainty, and anxiety that are suppressed in many young people about this issue. This TalkSheet provides a forum for positive discussion on nuclear war and the role of Christians as peacemakers.

OPENER

To start this discussion, break the group into four smaller groups placed strategically around the room. Give each group its own table and tell them each table represents a country. Place a larger table in the middle of the room to represent the United Nations.

Any country can send a representative to any other country by going to another's table. Give each group an envelope that contains information about its country. Keep the information brief, but mention the number of nuclear weapons it has, the wealth it possesses, and the level of democracy that exists. Be sure to designate one country as a primarily Christian nation. Tape a list of each country's information on the United Nations table for all the countries to see. Give each country one minute to talk briefly about its information and to select a president, an ambassador to each other country, and a United Nations representative.

Announce that one of the countries has been attacked by another with nuclear weapons. Tape a damage list with the name of the attacking country to the attacked country's table. Then let the game begin by allowing the attacked country as well as the other countries to decide what they will do about the situation.

THE DISCUSSION, BY NUMBERS

1. This generation of young people tends to be pessimistic about the future. Depending on the most current world crisis, young people will usually predict the use of at least one nuclear weapon during their lifetime. What do your students think?

2. Young people can come up with any number of possibilities. Ask them if any of their potential scenarios are positive ones. How many of them involve massive destruction? Are any of them inevitable? Are there ways that we as Christians can work to avert them?

3. Examine the issue of when (if ever) it would be morally right to use nuclear weapons. U.S. President Harry Truman was the first human being to have the power and the weight of this decision on his shoulders.

4. What do your kids think? Do they disagree on any of these statements? Why or why not?

5. Let volunteers share their answers and give reasons for their responses. Then talk about the many ways young people cope with the threat of nuclear war. For example, hedonism (an attitude of living for today); trust (a feeling that those in control will use good judgment); denial (a refusal to think about it much); indestructibility (a feeling that it could never happen); and postmodern progress (a belief that we have learned from the past and won't use nuclear weapons). Discuss with the group how Christ offers hope in the midst of despair.

6. You may want to divide the group into three smaller ones and assign each a different passage of the Bible. Each group should discuss a passage and report its conclusions.

THE CLOSE

Fears and concerns about the growth in nuclear weapons and the threat of war are normal. But God is in control of nations. If you survey the Old Testament, you'll clearly see that God was in control of history—even though it didn't always appear that way to his people. Encourage your kids to pray for the powerful countries of the world and for wisdom of world leaders. You may want to close by reading the Beatitudes from the Sermon on the Mount (Matthew 5:1-12), emphasizing verse nine. Contrast Christ's teachings of peacemaking with the way nuclear-capable countries run their foreign policies.

MORE

● You may want to ask your kids to make a list of all the movies they've seen in which nuclear war was a threat. Does your group think that these movies accurately describe the threat of war? Why or why not? What influence do they think media has on how people think of war and nuclear weapons?

● Check out some online information about nuclear war and weapons. There are several Web pages with simulation maps and more. Challenge your kids to find some new information about nuclear war by doing a keyword search of nuclear war or check out http://www.pbs.org/wgbh/amex/bomb/.

THINK IT THROUGH

1. What are **two problems** that all teenagers have to face?

2. What do you think? Are these statements **R (really true)**, **S (sort of true)**, or **N (not really true)**?

___ When Christians have problems in their lives, they should let God decide what to do.

___ Your Christian beliefs don't make much difference when looking for solutions to everyday problems.

___ Christians shouldn't think much about problems they face, since it's God's job to tell them what to do.

___ A Christian should work with God to solve life's problems.

___ When a tough situation is encountered, young people should figure out what it means on their own.

___ God wants to work with us on every problem we face.

___ When Christians are upset, they should ask God to take the anxious feelings away.

___ When faced with a problem, you're better off going with the feelings you have and not trying to lean on God.

___ God can help a Christian figure out solutions to life's problems.

___ God will somehow work out Christians' problems for them.

___ Rather than tell God our problems, we should take action to work them out.

___ We can work hard to solve life's problems, because we know God is working with us.

___ Christians should trust the Lord to give them the answers to their problems.

3. Put an arrow by the statement that best describes how you handle your problems.
God solves all my problems
I let everyone else (parents, teachers, friends) deal with my problems.
I deal with problems alone—I don't even tell God my problems.
I ignore my problems.

4. The following are three examples of how biblical believers looked at problems. Pick one to read and then write down what the verses say in your own words.
Exodus 4:10-12
Nehemiah 2:2-5
2 Corinthians 1:8-11

From *More High School TalkSheets—Updated!* by David Lynn. Permission to reproduce this page granted only for use in the buyer's own youth group. www.YouthSpecialties.com

51

THINK IT THROUGH [problem solving]

THIS WEEK

This TalkSheet lets you and your high schoolers examine how they approach their problems—both big and small. Do they solve them themselves, expect God to solve all of them, or cooperate with God in working out their problems?

Be aware that some kids in your group may be dealing with some massive problems in their lives, including alcoholism, premarital sex, depression, physical or sexual abuse, divorce at home, pornography, and more. Pay close attention to the dynamics of your group throughout this discussion.

OPENER

Before you start, write some problem scenarios on pieces of paper. Feel free to expand on this list, leave any out, or add any that you think of—these are to help you get started.

- You're not doing well in classes and your parents are angry. But you're trying your hardest.
- Your friend started dating a guy (or girl) two months ago and now he (or she) wants to have sex. Your friend isn't sure if she should.
- You found out that your closest friend has started using drugs.
- A teammate has been coming to school with bruises on her face, arms, and legs. She says she fell during track practice, but you and your teammates know her dad has a hot temper.
- Your friend's mom was diagnosed with cancer. She may live only a few months.
- You've been cut from the basketball team and now your so-called friends on the team have ditched you.
- You just aren't fitting in at school—you've tried to dress cool, be nice, and all that. But it hasn't worked.
- You've come home on Friday to find your parents screaming at each other. They've been fighting a lot—and you heard your dad threaten to leave.

Split your kids into groups and give each group a problem. Then ask them to read the problem and think about how they would handle the situation—realistically. What would the implications be if they made different decisions? How often have your kids heard of situations like these?

THE DISCUSSION, BY NUMBERS

1. Write down all the suggestions. What are the most common problems of teenagers? Which one does your group think is the most common?

2. How do your kids respond to these statements? Take some time to talk about the validity of each of these. What do they say about Christians and problems? What have your kids been brought up to believe about God and dealing with their problems?

3. As a follow-up to question 2, how do your kids handle their problems? In general, who do they turn to the most—themselves, others, or God? What do they find the most comfort in? Why or why not?

4. Let different individuals share their reflections from each of the three situations. You may want to conclude by reflecting on Romans 8:28.

THE CLOSE

Remind your group that God is a partner in problem solving. Most Christians would probably agree that God and his people work together—he guides and enables them to solve problems. Emphasize to your kids that God is able to help solve problems. But they need to be willing to come to him with their problems and concerns and trust that he is able to handle them!

Encourage your kids to find a trusted adult to talk with—including you, if they feel comfortable. Stress that it is vital for them to get help in dealing with these problems. If you sense it's appropriate, you may want close in prayer with your group.

For more information and links to specific Web sites and resources, check out lessons www.X-rated.sin (page 87), Hooked on Drugs (page 61), and Your Last Breath (page 101).

MORE

- You may want to continue this discussion with a Q&A with your group. Ask your kids to write down problems they are struggling with. (Be sure to keep it anonymous.) Then collect the problems and read them individually to the group. Be sure to screen them for appropriateness before you read them out loud. Then have your group to brainstorm solutions to the problems. What advice do they have for each other? How can God help in the situations? What are some tangible solutions for finding answers?
- What are some ways that that TV and movie characters deal with problems? You may want to show a clip of a TV show or movie and then talk with the group about how the character(s) handled a problem. What was effective and not effective? Why or why not? What does advice does society have for dealing with problems? Are these healthy solutions or not? Point out to your group that many people deal with their problems in unhealthy ways—turning to drugs, alcohol, or physical abuse, to deal with their problems.

BUY NOW, PAY LATER

1. How much stuff do you think today's teenagers want compared to what teens might have wanted in past generations? Why or why not?

2. You've completed your education and are working. How important is it for you to own each of the following items?

   V (very important)   **N (not really important)**

   S (somewhat important)   **D (definitely not important)**

   ___ A new car or truck   ___ A VCR or DVD player   ___ A microwave oven
   ___ A big-screen TV   ___ A recreational vehicle   ___ A car stereo system
   ___ A home computer   ___ A pager   ___ A video game system
       with Internet access   ___ A home   ___ A cordless phone
   ___ A laptop computer   ___ A stereo system
   ___ A cell phone   ___ A fashionable
                            wardrobe

3. Rank the following things from what you would **most likely spend your money on (1)** to what you would **least likely spend your money on (7)**.

   ___ Stuff for personal use
   ___ Helping others
   ___ Going out and having a good time
   ___ Saving for further education
   ___ Helping with family expenses
   ___ Tithing
   ___ A girlfriend or boyfriend

4. Read these statements and decide whether they're **T (true)** or **F (false)** for you.

   ___ Teens will want less as they accumulate more.
   ___ Teens will have a higher standard of living than their parents.
   ___ Teens should be given the material things they want.
   ___ Teens worry about having enough money in the future, more than anything else.
   ___ Teens want and expect stuff based on what their families want and expect.
   ___ Teens who have more stuff are more popular.
   ___ Teens can have too many possessions.
   ___ Teens must give up their possessions to follow Christ.

5. Read the following Bible verses and write what they say about God's perspective regarding money and possessions.

   Proverbs 8:10   Isaiah 55:2   Matthew 16:24-26   Luke 12:15
   Proverbs 30:8, 9   Amos 6:1, 4-7   Luke 6:38

From *More High School TalkSheets—Updated!* by David Lynn. Permission to reproduce this page granted only for use in the buyer's own youth group. www.YouthSpecialties.com

BUY NOW, PAY LATER [materialism and consumerism]

THIS WEEK

There's no doubt that consumerism has infected our society—and affected the youth culture as well. The media has influenced the expectations of young people, whether they're poor, middle class, or rich. Teens between the ages of 12-17 spend over $100 billion annually—that's over $4,400 each*! Is this consumerism acceptable by Christian standards? And how do your churched kids handle their money surrounded by a mentality that says they need it all? This TalkSheet explores the topic of possessions and materialistic values and how your kids can avoid getting caught in the urge to buy now, pay later.

OPENER

See if your kids realize how much money is spent on them—give each person a piece of paper and something to write with, then have them make a list of all the stuff they have on their bodies. They should list all that they're wearing—including what's in their wallets, pockets, and purses. Have them include things like glasses, contact lenses, and braces. Next to each item they should write down an estimate of how much each item costs to calculate the total worth of what they're wearing. Then add up the individual totals and write down the total for the whole group. You and your kids may be surprised at the amount of money that has been spent on the group members! Point out that this amount could be more than the annual income of families in third world countries. Pretty scary, huh?

THE DISCUSSION, BY NUMBERS

1. In the past young people didn't have as much because there wasn't as much to have. Today, a person could fill a warehouse full of consumer goods. What do your kids think?

2. Here you will get at the kids' material expectations. Ask them why they plan to own the things they identified. How can the things they want get in the way of their relationship with God? How much stuff is enough?

3. This activity identifies the priorities of your students. Have the kids guess how Jesus might rank these, and compare the two lists.

4. Ask the students to share their choices and their reasons why. Take some time to discuss them if some are debatable within your group.

5. In the Bible, Christ had much to say about money and possessions. Some of the Bible passages are very straightforward. Other passages sound contradictory. Examine them and decide which make

the most sense and which seem to be paradoxes. Come to some conclusions about God's view of possessions and money. Ask the group to decide which (if any) of these passages are lived out by the average person in our society.

THE CLOSE

Remind the group of the introductory activity, and challenge them to convince a teenager from an average third world country that the youth group is not wealthy—hard to do, considering how much stuff even poor teenage Americans have!

In the past people had less stuff than we do now. Closet space savers, storage sheds, and rental storage space have increased our ability to consume by giving us more places to put things. We can consume and consume endlessly, always wanting and getting more. God says, however, that you must give in order to get; you must lose your life to save it. Christ repeatedly warned his disciples about the dangers of possessions—they get in the way of living life! It isn't necessarily the stuff itself that gets us into trouble, but our attitude toward it! Jesus warned us against the belief that our possessions will provide us with happiness.

Consider closing with the parable of the sower found in Matthew 13:1-23, focusing especially on verse 22.

MORE

● Why not raise money for those who don't have what they need, let alone what they want? Consider doing a fundraiser, clothing drive, food drive, or some other activity to help a charity or other organization. You may want to plan a garage sale or church rummage sale for people to sell those things that they don't want or need. Then donate the money and left over items.

● How do advertisements affect materialism and consumerism? Ask your kids to make a list of everywhere they see advertisements—on clothing, on buses, on the Internet, and even on cereal boxes. Where do they see advertising? How does advertising influence people to buy things they don't need? How can your kids keep advertisements from getting to them?

* Teen Fact Book 2000, Channel One Network: New York, Los Angeles, Chicago. Used by permission.

PARENT'S V.S. PEER'S

Note: The term parent in the following items refers to all kinds of parenting adults—birth, step, foster, or guardian.

1. **Do you agree with this statement?**
Most teenagers rebel against their parents or guardians.

2. **How often do you think teenagers in general rebel against their parents?**
   - ❑ All of the time
   - ❑ Most of the time
   - ❑ Some of the time
   - ❑ None of the time

3. **Do you think this statement is true for you?**
The more heavily involved teenagers become with their peer group, the more likely they will not accept a parent's values and beliefs.

   What about teenagers in general?

4. **Who would you go to for advice on the following—P (parents) or F (friends)?**

   ___ What classes to take at school
   ___ What sports to play
   ___ Whether or not to drink or use drugs
   ___ What to do about a small personal problem
   ___ What to do about big personal problems
   ___ How to spend your free time
   ___ How to choose good friends
   ___ How to style your hair
   ___ What time to be home on weekend nights
   ___ If you had concerns regarding sexual issues.

   ___ What to pursue as a career after high school
   ___ What TV shows to watch
   ___ Who to go out with
   ___ How to spend your money
   ___ What music to listen to
   ___ How involved to be at church
   ___ How to dress
   ___ Whether or not to attend college
   ___ Whether or not to work in high school
   ___ How to deal with others

5. **Place an X on the scale below near the point that best describes you.**

   My parents have a major influence on my values.   My parents have little influence on my values.

6. **Each of the following passages of the Bible touches on the issue of influence. Write a short sentence that describes how each one applies to parent versus peer influence today.**
   Genesis 6:9, 10; 7:1   1 Samuel 2:22-25   Matthew 5:13
   Genesis 13:12, 13   2 Kings 15:8, 9

From *More High School TalkSheets—Updated!* by David Lynn. Permission to reproduce this page granted only for use in the buyer's own youth group. www.YouthSpecialties.com

PARENTS VS. PEERS [influence of parents and friends]

THIS WEEK

Parents or guardians of teenagers worry about a number of things—peer group influence is usually one of them. Your responsibilities as a youth leader include affirming the role parents play in the lives of young people. At the same time, you are also called to help kids live in the world of their peers. Use this TalkSheet to talk about the role of parents and peers in the lives of the young people in your group.

Be sensitive to those kids who may not have good relationships with the adults in their lives. Some of your group members may come from broken homes or may not live with their parents.

OPENER

To start this discussion, place two chairs facing each other in the front or the middle of the room. Print the word PARENT on a paper and tape it to one of the chairs. Put the word PEER on another chair. Then you can either ask for volunteers to come up and take turns sitting in the chairs or let your kids take turns coming up to sit in the chairs.

Tell your kids that each chair represents either a parent or a peer perspective—they could be the same or different, depending on the issue. Give the volunteers a topic to debate from both a parent and a peer viewpoint. These topics could include dating, allowance, bad grades, curfew, getting grounded, church attendance, homework, music, and chores. The person who sits in each chair should take either a parent or a peer point of view.

THE DISCUSSION, BY NUMBERS

1. Keep this on a feeling level. Do kids feel comfortable, uncomfortable, anxious, excited, nervous, angry, or happy? Ask the students to give examples that illustrate why they feel the way they do.

2. Let young people respond to the statement, then have the group reach a consensus. You may want to reverse the question—are parents anti-teenagers? How about adults in general? Does this affect how young people accept adult values and beliefs?

3. Many in your group will say this hasn't been true in their lives. Most kids don't believe that peer pressure affects them inside. They feel they are unique individuals and make up their own minds.

4. After kids share some of their responses, ask the group to summarize a basic statement about this issue. For example, the more important and far-reaching the issue, the more likely the young person will be influenced by parents. Or, the older

someone gets the more likely they are to listen to peers over parents.

5. Ask questions like whether or not parents should influence our values, why parents want to influence our values, and who will influence our values if parents don't.

6. Let the young people share what they discovered. Focus on Matthew 5:13 and ask how Christian young people can influence both their parents and their peers. This introduces a more proactive slant to the discussion so that your students become active influencers rather than passive objects of influence.

THE CLOSE

God isn't against friends or parents. He has offered some guidelines in the Bible not as killjoy principles, but as a road map to guide kids. Read Proverbs 1:8-19 and tell the group that this is only one guideline that must be balanced with others. Generally speaking, they can rely on their parents for the important things in life, and they must weigh carefully what their friends say.

MORE

● How does the media influence how your kids think of parents versus peers? Ask your kids a few of these questions and see how they respond—
⇨ Do most TV shows promote parents or peers? Which shows promote parents or peers?
⇨ What do magazines (like Seventeen or Mademoiselle) emphasize more—parents or peers? How?
⇨ What movies have you seen lately that promote parental or peer relationships?
⇨ How about advertisements? Do your kids normally see advertisements for kids their age with parents or peers in them?
What conclusions can your group make based on the media? Is your society pro-parent or pro-peer? How do these influence your kids' relationships with parents and peers?

● You may want to plan an event or meeting with your kids and their parents. Or have your kids talk about one issue with their parents this week. Challenge them to take one topic or situation from the intro and ask their parents about. Did their parents handle it the same way the group did in the intro? Why or why not? What other input did their parents have? Do your group members feel differently about their parents?

THE AFTERLIFE

1. When you hear about the **afterlife**, what is the first thing you think about?

2. What do you think about these statements—do you **A (agree)** or **D (disagree)**?
___ People who live good lives will go to heaven.
___ Reincarnation makes as much sense as heaven.
___ There's no good reason to believe there is a hell.
___ Christians talk more about hell than they do about heaven.
___ There is no hell.
___ Hell won't be as bad a place as the Bible or pastors say it is.
___ The average young person believes in a heaven more than a hell.
___ Talking about hell will scare people into wanting to know more about how to get to heaven.
___ Christians should be more worried about the here and now than about the afterlife.
___ If there is a heaven, there must be a hell.
___ The belief in heaven keeps people from seeking happiness on earth.

3. Do you think that life in heaven will be more like or less like life on earth?

   Why?

4. How can a person's views about heaven and hell affect the way they live their life?

5. Check out these verses and write what each passage has to say about heaven or hell.
   Matthew 25:46   Philippians 1:23, 24
   Luke 16:24-26   2 Peter 2:4-9
   1 Corinthians 1:18

From *More High School TalkSheets—Updated!* by David Lynn. Permission to reproduce this page granted only for use in the buyer's own youth group. www.YouthSpecialties.com

THE AFTERLIFE [heaven and hell]

THIS WEEK

The Bible provides only glimpses of what heaven and hell will be like. But it clearly teaches that both exist. Even people who don't hold to religious beliefs express interest in the afterlife. Talk shows have guests who claim to have died and seen the afterlife, magazines write about people who claim they have lived before and will do so again, and opinion polls report people's views regarding the afterlife. This TalkSheet encourages a group examination of both heaven and hell.

OPENER

To start, have your kids split into groups and find more information on heaven and hell throughout the Bible. Give each group one of these verses—

Revelation 4:1-6	Revelation 21:15-21
Revelation 4:6-11	Revelation 21:22-27
Revelation 5:1-5	Revelation 22:1-5
Revelation 5:6-14	Matthew 8:12
Revelation 6:8	Luke 16:19-31
Revelation 7:16-17	Matthew 25:41
Revelation 19:1-10	2 Peter 2:4
Revelation 20:10-15	Jude 1:6
Revelation 21:1-8	2 Thessalonians 1:9
Revelation 21:9-14	Mark 12:25-27

Have your groups read these verses and then write down or summarize what each set of verses says about either heaven or hell. You may want to have volunteers read different verses out loud and then talk about the verses with your group. What new understanding of heaven or hell do they have? What realities of both heaven and hell are given here?

THE DISCUSSION, BY NUMBERS

1. Allow students to share their thoughts about the afterlife. Pay particular attention to how your group has been influenced by secular views: there is no hell, the afterlife will be boring, reincarnation really happens, and so on.

2. Take a poll on each of the statements. If there is a difference of opinion, encourage a debate on their ideas. Does believing in heaven and hell keep Christians from serving God and others on earth?

3. People often think of heaven as blissful nothingness where we sit on clouds and talk about God. Yet the Bible speaks of real streets and actual work for God. Heaven is a very real place. Paul spoke of seeing things as a poor reflection in a mirror, but in heaven we shall see things as they really are (1 Corinthians 13:12).

4. What do your students think about earthly life versus heavenly life? In what ways to they think heaven may be like earth or not like earth? As the students share their answers, you may want to use 2 Peter 3:11-13 as a reference.

5. The Bible doesn't tell us everything we'd like to know about heaven and hell, but it does give us glimpses of both. Have the students share what they learned about heaven and hell and their attitudes toward them.

THE CLOSE

Heaven and hell are a reality—the Bible tells us that both are real. God has given every person a choice—to love him and serve him, or not to. Your kids might ask why a loving God would condemn anyone to hell. But the real question is why would anyone want to reject God's love? God wants everyone to experience eternal life with him (John 5:24; 2 Peter 3:9). And each person is bound for one or the other (Ecclesiastes 12:13, 14). Point out that this lesson is not meant to scare them into believing in Jesus—but it is information that they should know. Let them know that you are willing to talk with them one-on-one if any of them have questions or other concerns.

MORE

- You may want to show some clips of a movie that portrays heaven or hell. Or ask your kids to brainstorm a list of movies and TV shows that have dealt with the afterlife. Need some suggestions? Try "What Dreams May Come" (PolyGram Films) and "Ghost" (Paramount Pictures). Also check out more movie reviews and summaries at www.hollywoodjesus.com.

  After you watch part of the movie or talk with your kids about movies (or TV shows) they've seen, ask them a few questions. How did the characters deal with heaven or hell? What happened in the movie? Do your kids think these are accurate representations of heaven or hell? Why or why not? What have your kids heard differently in church or in school? What is different and why?

- You might want to have your senior pastor and a few other adults come into the meeting to help answer the questions that your kids may have about heaven and hell. No one knows all the answers, but your group might like to hear outside ideas and ask questions, too.

SEEKING THE TRUTH

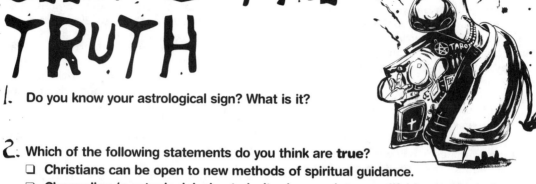

1. Do you know your astrological sign? What is it?

2. Which of the following statements do you think are **true**?
   - ❑ Christians can be open to new methods of spiritual guidance.
   - ❑ Channeling (a satanic delusion to invite demons into your life) is extremely dangerous.
   - ❑ Christians shouldn't watch shows or movies that deal with spiritual trends.
   - ❑ Reading horoscopes and talking with psychics isn't that risky.
   - ❑ The New Age movement is more popular than Christianity in our country.
   - ❑ Satan and his demons can't get involved in the lives of Christians.
   - ❑ More people read their horoscopes every day than read the Bible every day.
   - ❑ The church is responsible for getting people involved in a variety of spiritual orientations today.

3. Put an arrow by the three that interest you the most.
   I would like to learn what the Bible teaches about—

The New Age movement	Satanism	Magic
Reincarnation	Eastern mysticism	Tarot cards
Astrology	Crystal power	Channeling
Feng shui	Psychic hotlines	Other—
Witchcraft	The occult	

4. Read the following Bible verses—what does each verse have to say about spiritual guidance?

   Psalm 48:14

   John 16:13

   Acts 17:22-27

   Ephesians 4:17, 18

   1 John 1:6

From *More High School TalkSheets—Updated!* by David Lynn. Permission to reproduce this page granted only for use in the buyer's own youth group. www.YouthSpecialties.com

SEEKING THE TRUTH [spiritual trends and false religions]

THIS WEEK

Many high schoolers have encountered crystals, psychics, horoscopes, witchcraft, false religions, and Eastern meditation techniques. TV, movies, the Internet, magazines, and music expose youth to these spiritual trends and false religions. This TalkSheet will give you an opportunity to talk about these spiritual counterfeits with your group.

Be sensitive to your group during this discussion. Some churches don't like to openly discuss these issues. And some of your kids may have been involved in this stuff or have friends who are involved. There is power in satanic spiritual trends—don't underestimate the other side! Your goal here isn't to encourage your kids in any way to explore these—but to talk about these trends in an informative way.

OPENER

Have a radio in front of you as you begin this activity. Demonstrate that your radio can provide you with different sources of information, entertainment, and news when you tune in to frequencies. When you tune in to different stations, you receive different broadcasts. And if a person isn't familiar with the stations, they'll have to search for program formats they like. Have your kids ever had to do that when they've been on vacation or in a different town? What happens if they don't know what to listen to? Do they keep searching until they find what they want? What makes them stay on a particular station? Probably the voice, the DJ, or the type of music that's played.

Then ask the group if they can see how the radio is like spiritual guidance. Point out that there's an abundance of spiritual counterfeits trying to get the attention of young people—broadcasting their lies and deceptions. Explain that many teens are tuning in to these counterfeits and need to know what the Bible has to say about it.

THE DISCUSSION, BY NUMBERS

1. This activity is not designed to excite or entice your kids into astrology. Rather it illustrates how familiar people are with it. Ask the group how astrology affects people today. Point out the psychic hotlines and the astrology guides in most newspapers and grocery stores. How many of your kids read theirs on a daily basis?

2. Expect debate and questions about each of these statements. You may want to discuss the availability of some of these practices. Why are there so many movies and television shows with supernatural themes that are borderline or outright satanic? Ask the kids which movies, television shows, and Internet sites are deceptive and dangerous and which are not. Do any present demons and the spirit world accurately, according to the Bible?

3. Is your group interested in learning more about these spiritual counterfeit movements? If so, you may want to pursue one or more within a Christian context. A lot of your kids may know of others who are involved in some of these practices. You may want to ask your senior pastor to help you in a later discussion about some of these items.

4. Ask the students to share their thoughts on what they learned from the Bible verses. How do these verses apply to their lives?

THE CLOSE

Looking for and wanting guidance is a normal part of life—especially for teenagers. Even the children of Israel continuously sought guidance—sometimes from God and other times from false gods and spiritual mediums. But God has promised to guide those who follow him (Psalm 31:3)—Christians have access to the infinite yet personal God of the Bible who's there all the time. You may want to close by reading Hebrews 13:9 and having a time of prayer.

For more information on the issues discussed, you may want to contact one of these organizations—Spiritual Counterfeit Projects (www.scp-inc.org), Christian Research Institute (www.equip.org), or the World Religions Index (http://wri.leaderu.com).

MORE

- The Bible is very clear about the power of Satan. With your group, find and read some verses in the Bible that talk about the power of Satan and the spiritual battle with Christians. A few include 1 Peter 5:8, James 4:7, 2 Timothy 2:26, and Ephesians 6:10-17. What do these verses say to Christians? What warnings does it give? How can Christians resist the devil and stand firm?

- On a poster board or whiteboard, write down the following (and any others you'd like to include)—horoscopes, Ouija boards, tarot cards, psychic hotlines, dream discussions and analysis, chants and deep meditation, hypnosis, palm reading.

    Ask your group if they know what each of these are? What does each one test or reveal? Do they know people who are involved in using one or more of these? Are there any more that aren't on the list? How reliable or powerful are these practices? How accurate are each of these for telling the truth?

HOOKED ON DRUGS

1. Circle from the list below the **five drugs** most frequently used by teenagers.

Caffeine	Heroin	Alcohol
LSD	Speed	Downers
Tobacco	Inhalants	Other—
Marijuana	Cocaine	

2. Why do you think the five drugs you circled are used the most by teenagers?

3. Rank the following from the **best reason (1)** to the **worst reason (8)** for you to avoid alcohol and other drugs.

   ❏ To avoid addiction
   ❏ To remain close to God
   ❏ To not lose good friends
   ❏ To keep from disappointing parents

   ❏ To avoid getting into trouble
   ❏ To reduce problems in the future
   ❏ To avoid violation of personal values
   ❏ To prevent physical harm

4. Is this statement true for you? Why or why not?
   Alcohol and other drugs have become easier for me to avoid as I have gotten older.

5. Write a one-sentence summary of how each of the following Bible verses applies to the issues of drinking and doing drugs.

   Proverbs 21:16, 17

   Romans 14:13-18

   1 Corinthians 3:16, 17

   1 Corinthians 10:23, 24

From *More High School TalkSheets—Updated!* by David Lynn. Permission to reproduce this page granted only for use in the buyer's own youth group. www.YouthSpecialties.com

HOOKED ON DRUGS [substance abuse]

THIS WEEK

Alcohol and other drug use is an issue that remains problematic in society. Make no mistake, alcohol is a drug. This isn't to suggest that adults shouldn't drink in moderation. But those adults, as well as young people, need to understand that when they drink they are consuming a legal drug. Take the opportunity to talk with your young people about drugs and how they can avoid them.

Be sensitive to those in your group who may have been using drugs already. According to statistics, there most likely are a few in your group who have experimented. Be careful not to come off sounding judgmental—keep an open mind during the discussion.

OPENER

Ask the students to name all the celebrities they know of (athletes, actors, musicians, politicians, and so on) who have had problems with alcohol or drugs. You will be able to create a long list of names. Ask the group if they know why any of these supposedly successful individuals became involved in substance abuse. Then discuss the consequences of that involvement. Did it affect their careers? Who went to jail? Who divorced or lost their children as a result of their dependency? Who lost their lives? Finally, ask the students if these individuals make substance abuse glamorous to teens. This will lead directly into your first TalkSheet question.

THE DISCUSSION, BY NUMBERS

1. Generally speaking, the three most frequently used drugs are caffeine, tobacco, and alcohol. Point out that these three are addictive drugs even though they are legal.

2. Create a master list of reasons why these drugs are used by teenagers. What makes them want to use? What are the rewards of doing drugs? How do they initially get hooked?

3. Here the group can focus on good reasons to avoid use. Reach a group consensus on the best reasons to avoid use. What makes it hard to resist using drugs in today's society?

4. Has it gotten easier for your kids to resist drugs and alcohol? Most likely not. Spend some time talking about peers and media influences. Why is it harder to resist than before? What can your kids do to stay clean, despite the pressures?

5. Let students share their various perspectives on the passages. Focus on one or two passages of interest to the group.

THE CLOSE

The temptations to use drugs are everywhere. As you close, don't lecture your kids—affirm them. It takes will power and determination to stay clean. Encourage them to find others to support them—to keep them accountable for saying no. And point out that God gives power to those who ask for help in resisting temptation—check out 1 Corinthians 10:13 or James 1:12-15. Challenge your kids to make a commitment to stay clean and to find someone who can encourage them.

MORE

● How can your kids deal with addiction? What if they have a friend who is hooked? What can they do to help themselves and others? You may want to talk more about how to handle drug abuse and the importance of breaking the addiction. For information and discussion ideas, check out the National Council on Alcoholism and Drug Dependence, Inc. (http://ncadd.org) or the Addiction Research Foundation (www.arf.org/isd/info.html). You may want to talk about the effects of alcohol and drug abuse on families—some of your kids may face abusive homes or alcoholic family members. These are real issues that need attention. What are the signs of an addicted parent or sibling? Where can your kids go to find help and encouragement?

● Or you may want to ask someone to talk about drug addiction—possibly someone who works with users, treats those who are addicted, or has recovered from drug abuse. Some of your kids may have stories of people that they know who have been hooked. Take some time to talk about these stories and what happened—but be sure to mediate the conversation. What did your kids learn from these stories? How real are the dangers of drugs and alcohol?

DIFFERENT OR DISABLED?

1. Circle each of the following conditions that you would consider a major disability.

Drug addiction	Blindness	Mental illness
Down syndrome	Alzheimer's	Paraplegia
Cancer	Autism	Ulcer
Allergies	An amputated arm	Speech impediment
Learning disabilities	Schizophrenia	Asthma
Diabetes	ADHD	Facial birthmark
Epilepsy	Cerebral palsy	Cleft palate or harelip
Spina bifida	Obesity	
Deafness	A permanent limp	

2. Put an arrow by the conditions in question 1 that you think kids at your school would be least accepting of.

3. How would you finish these statements?

Most people handicap (or limit)
people with disabilities by—

I handicap (or limit) people with disabilities by—

4. What do you think—**Y (yes)** or **N (no)**?

___ Teenagers who have disabilities usually aren't accepted by people their age.

___ People aren't attractive if they have disabilities.

___ Some disabilities are more socially crippling than others.

___ Some people with disabilities have special traits or talents that other people don't have.

___ It's fair that people with disabilities are given special privileges or exceptions.

___ Teenagers with disabilities have the right to the same opportunities as those who don't have disabilities.

___ Women are more accepting of people with disabilities than men.

___ It's likely for a person to develop a disability—not just be born with one.

___ The media fairly portrays people with disabilities

___ The more contact you have with a person who has a disability, the more accepting you are of people with disabilities.

___ People with disabilities are usually unhappy.

5. Read two of the Bible verse groupings below and write out how they apply to disabilities.
Job 5:7; Job 14:1, 2; Isaiah 40:6-8—
Romans 8:18; 2 Corinthians 4:17; 2 Timothy 2:10—
Psalm 119:49, 50; 2 Corinthians 1:3, 4—
Isaiah 40:31; 2 Corinthians 12:9, 10; Ephesians 3:16, 17—
Isaiah 60:20; Revelation 7:17; Revelation 21:4—

From *More High School TalkSheets—Updated!* by David Lynn. Permission to reproduce this page granted only for use in the buyer's own youth group. www.YouthSpecialties.com

DIFFERENT OR DISABLED? [disabilities]

THIS WEEK

Teenagers are often ignorant of the difficulties encountered by people who have disabilities. Some show their ignorance and discomfort by making fun of the disable or looking down on them. This TalkSheet offers the opportunity to discuss what it means to have a disability and how Christians should respond.

OPENER

How does the media treat people with disabilities? How do TV shows or movies portray physical or mental disabilities? Why do the media and other people shy away from dealing with these issues? Why do advertisements show only perfect, healthy people to sell their products? Why are there so few TV shows with disabled characters in them? What do your kids think about how the media handles these? Is it healthy for our culture or not? Does it help educate the public?

THE DISCUSSION, BY NUMBERS

1. Other words unfortunately sometimes used to describe those with disabilities are infirm, shut-in, defective, handicapped, deformed, and disabled. Point out to the group that we need to use the phrase "people with disabilities" rather than the disabled, the handicapped, or the crippled. Discuss the myth that disability equals inability, which is simply not true.

2. Many teenagers aren't informed about these conditions. So you may want to be prepared to define each of these. Information can go a long way in helping young people become more compassionate and caring.

    For more information on these conditions, check out the National Health Information Center (http://nhic-nt.health.org), The National Information Center for Children and Youth with Disabilities (http://nichcy.org), Christian Counsel on Persons with Disabilities (www.ccpd.org), or search any search engine with the keyword *disabilities* for hundreds of links to more information.

3. Why are some disabilities more accepted than others? Why are some treated worse than others? Brainstorm how Christians can influence others to be more accepting of those with disabilities.

4. Explain that a disability is a condition, and a handicap is something that keeps a person from doing something. Ask the group to identify how attitudes and actions handicap people with disabilities. Have the kids list the ways people with disabilities are the same as everyone else.

5. Ask for a vote on each of the statements. Decide how young people with disabilities are discriminated against. What were their reactions to these? Are any of these myths?

6. Break the kids into groups and give each group some verses to look at. What conclusions did your kids reach from these verses?

THE CLOSE

Point out that people with disabilities are still people. They aren't patients—they aren't sick. People with disabilities need to be treated with dignity and respect. Too often others talk *for* them or *at* them, not *with* them. Thirdly, disability doesn't equal inability. Finally, emphasize that Christ died for all people—because he loves all people, regardless of mental or physical abilities—and he's called Christians to be compassionate to the disabled.

What different side of the disabled have your kids seen from this TalkSheet? What can your kids to do be compassionate and respectful of those with disabilities?

MORE

● The apostle Paul had a disability of some sort (2 Corinthians 12:7). In Galatians 6:11 the Bible gives a more specific hint regarding Paul's "thorn in the flesh." Paul probably had some sort of eye disorder or disease that blurred his vision. Paul says he pleaded with the Lord to take away this problem but the Lord had a different plan. Read God's plan for Paul and his disability in 2 Corinthians 12:9. Then talk about this with your group. What was Paul's outlook on life? Did his "thorn" prevent him from serving God and spreading the Gospel? How can this story be an inspiration to your kids and others?

● Do you have someone with a disability in your church? You may want to ask them to come speak to your group. Encourage your kids to ask he or she some questions about how it feels to be limited physically. How do other people treat them? What would they like to change about how others look at them or treat them? How has the disability affected them or changed them?

"MY PARENTS SPLIT UP"

1. When you think of **divorce**, what usually comes to your mind?

2. Check the **three most common things** you think most teenagers experience when their parents divorce.

   - ❑ Getting angry at both parents
   - ❑ Low self-esteem
   - ❑ Stress from living with one parent
   - ❑ Depression
   - ❑ Resentment toward parent who's dating

   - ❑ Dealing with post-divorce money problems
   - ❑ Feelings of abandonment
   - ❑ Weird holidays
   - ❑ Parent visitation problems

   - ❑ Lower grades
   - ❑ Problems with drugs
   - ❑ Health problems
   - ❑ Anger toward God
   - ❑ Listening to one parent gripe about the other

3. What advice or response would you have for someone in these situations?

   a. "My dad left my mom and moved in with his girlfriend—now he expects me to treat this lady like she's someone special."

   b. "I want to live with my dad. When my parents divorced, my mom moved my little sister and me to another state. But we aren't getting along and it has been two years."

   c. "I feel like my dad has dumped me. Since my parents' divorce, I hardly ever see him. The first year he came around quite often. But not now. I can't figure out what I have done wrong. My mom says he'll never change."

   d. "My mom and dad expect me to be their messenger. They use me as a go-between for their arguments. I'm tired of being in the middle but I don't know what to do!"

   e. "I hate it that my mom is dating. She brings home the weirdest guys!"

4. What do you think? Are any of these true for you?
   - ❑ I'll probably get divorced someday.
   - ❑ I could never forgive my parents for getting divorced.
   - ❑ It isn't that big of a deal to handle your parents' divorce.
   - ❑ I feel like I could have stopped or could stop my parents from divorcing.
   - ❑ I would like my marriage to be like that of my parents.
   - ❑ Talking about a parent's divorce to people who care helps ease the pain of divorce.

5. Check out these verses—how do they apply to teenagers' dealing with divorce?
   Isaiah 66:13   Psalm 23:1-4
   Psalm 119:76   2 Corinthians 1:3

From *More High School TalkSheets—Updated!* by David Lynn. Permission to reproduce this page granted only for use in the buyer's own youth group. www.YouthSpecialties.com

"MY PARENTS SPLIT UP" [divorce]

THIS WEEK

This TalkSheet isn't about the right or wrong of divorce, or to judge those parents who may be split up or divorced. Teens aren't responsible for marital failure but they must live with its consequences. This discussion will help you understand the feelings of kids who are experiencing or have experienced a divorce. And it gives kids whose parents haven't divorced the chance to understand and empathize with the tragedy of a marital failure.

Be sensitive to your group members who may be dealing with divorce or split families. There are many unique family situations today—even within the church. Pay close attention to the dynamics of your group and mediate this discussion. Be careful not to sound accusatory or judgmental—and don't let your kids get away with it either.

OPENER

For this intro, you'll need five photocopies of a marriage certificate, one frame, and some tape. Place one of the certificates into the frame, poke one with holes, tear one in several places, tear one into pieces and tape it back together again, and save one to be torn. Now hold the certificates up before the group. Explain that each of these certificates represents a marriage—

- The framed certificate is the picture-perfect marriage—the husband and wife care for each other and work hard at keeping the marriage together.
- The certificate with holes represents a marriage with some problems—there are a few difficulties eating away at it, but so far it's stayed together.
- The one torn in several places represents a hurting marriage—perhaps with help it will survive, or it may end in divorce.
- The certificate torn into pieces but taped together again represents a marriage that has been torn apart but is healing—there are scars, but it can still last.
- Finally, the last certificate should be held up and torn to pieces. This represents a marriage that has ended in divorce—the certificate of marriage no longer means anything.

THE DISCUSSION, BY NUMBERS

1. Ask the young people to speak up with their thoughts and then write each contribution on the whiteboard or on newsprint.

2. This lets kids who've experienced the pain share some of it with the rest of the group. Ask several of the students whose parents have divorced to share their answers, but be sensitive to those who may not be ready to discuss the issue in front of the group.

3. You may want to role-play these situations so that your students practice their peer counseling and support skills. But what would your kids say to others in these situations? How do teenagers in general deal with these situations?

4. How do your kids respond to these? What legitimate reasons do they have for their answers? Take some time to talk about these and why teenagers hold some of these ideas.

5. What do these verses say about dealing with divorce? Take some time to talk about God's comfort during challenging times with families.

THE CLOSE

For a close, use this activity to illustrate the high divorce rate in today's society. Sit with your group in a circle so they can see you flipping a coin (or you can have your kids take turns flipping the coin). As you (or the kids) flip the coin, have them call heads or tails. If they lose the toss, have them leave the circle. Continue this until everyone in your group has called a coin toss (or some of them, if your group is too big). Explain that this activity is like marriage and divorce—roughly half of all marriages in the U.S. end in divorce. The people outside of the circle represent those whose marriages failed. You may want to mention that—statistically—if they marry again, their chance of another divorce is even higher.

What fears or questions do your kids have about divorce? What does God think about divorce? Remind them that no one is judging those who are divorced—only God knows and understands each situation. Encourage your kids to find an adult to talk with if they are angry with their parents—but point out that their parents need love and support, too. Close with a time of prayer for your kids and their families.

MORE

- You may want to assemble a group of four to five people for a panel discussion on divorce—a divorced person, an adult child of divorce, a Christian counselor or pastor, and a married couple. Have your group members write questions for the panel—in advance if possible. What scares your group about marriage and divorce? How can they prepare themselves today for healthy marriages?
- Has the media influenced the divorce rate? Undoubtedly. You may want to take some time to talk about media influences with your kids. What do TV shows and movies say about divorce? How is separation and divorce portrayed? What affect does pornography have on marriages? What does music today say about divorce and splitting up? Does the media condone cheating on partners? How? Discuss each of these with your group and ask for specific examples that they may have.

THE GENESIS 1 QUESTION

1. Think about evolution and creation and answer the following questions.

    What makes the **most sense** to you about the theory of evolution?

    What makes the **least sense** to you about the theory of evolution?

    What makes the **most sense** to you about the theory of creation?

    What makes the **least sense** to you about the theory of creation?

2. What do you think—**Y (yes)** or **N (no)**?
    ___ An open-minded person has to accept evolution as truth.
    ___ The Bible and evolution are compatible.
    ___ Schools should teach both creation and evolution as theories in their science courses.
    ___ The Bible provides Christians with a scientific account of the origin of the world.
    ___ A person can't be a Christian and still believe in evolution.
    ___ Christians shouldn't study science.

3. Answer each of the following questions the way you think the Bible teaches and then the way you think science teaches.

    a. Is there a God?
    The Bible says—
    Science says—

    b. How was the world formed?
    The Bible says—
    Science says—

    c. How unique are people?
    The Bible says—
    Science says—

    d. How do the laws of nature work?
    The Bible says—
    Science says—

4. Each of the following statements summarizes a belief about the origin of life. Choose the one that comes closest to what you believe.
    ❑ Life evolved through naturalistic processes over a long period of time with no creator involved.
    ❑ God made life, then allowed it to evolve through naturalistic processes over a long period of time.
    ❑ God made life and directed its evolution toward a purpose over a long period of time.
    ❑ God made life as it exists today and designed all of it for a special purpose.

5. Check out each of the following verses that describe God in relationship to the world and everything in it. What does each of these passages suggest how people should interpret scientific data?
    Psalm 19:1-6   2 Peter 3:13
    Colossians 1:16, 17   Revelation 14:7

From *More High School TalkSheets—Updated!* by David Lynn. Permission to reproduce this page granted only for use in the buyer's own youth group. www.YouthSpecialties.com

THE GENESIS 1 QUESTION [science and creation]

THIS WEEK

Christian young people in public schools are confronted with questions and doubts about the validity of their religious faith when it appears to conflict with their science classes. This TalkSheet encourages an open and honest discussion on the subject of science and creation.

This may be a sensitive topic in some churches. It's important that you be familiar with the group's beliefs before starting this discussion. And be sure to create an environment of safety where the kids in your group can openly express their opinions and get concrete feedback from you or your leaders.

OPENER

To start, you may want to show a video on creation or evolution—or bring some articles, facts, or information to discuss with your group. You can find articles on creation versus evolution, critiques from scientists, engineers, archeologists, and more! Check out these Internet resources—the Creation Research Society (www.creationresearch.org), Answers in Genesis Ministries International (www.answersingenesis.org), Christian Answers Network (www.christiananswers.net), and Creation Science Home Page (http://emporium.turnpike.net /C/cs/index.htm).

Then ask your kids what they have learned in school about how the earth was created. Make a list of all the different ideas, theories, or stories that your kids have learned or heard about. Maybe ask a couple of them to bring in their school science textbooks to read bits on the creation story. Then read Genesis 1 to your group and ask them to listen closely while you read. How drastically do the two theories compare?

THE DISCUSSION, BY NUMBERS

1. Give volunteers the opportunity to share their answers. Keep the discussion participants from discounting or putting down the views of individuals.

2. Discuss each statement, allowing time for debate. Christianity focuses on the why and what should be, while science leans toward the how and what is. Science examines and tries to explain data—usually with competing theories, rather than one certain explanation!

3. The following are brief comments about each statement. (a) The Bible says there is a God who is both infinite and personal. Science says the existence of God can never be proved. (b) The Bible says God created the world fundamentally as it appears now except for the distortion sin has created. Science generally says that the world

evolved over millions and millions of years. (c) The Bible says that people have been created in the image of God, making them unique. Science says people are linked to all creation through an evolutionary process that makes all living things similar. (d) The Bible says God created and controls his laws of nature. Science says that nature is controlled by laws that aren't influenced by any outside force or power.

4. Allow the young people to share their views. If they come up with an additional view, ask them to write it on a whiteboard or on newsprint for everyone to examine.

5. Each passage describes God as the Creator. Explain to the group that all people interpret any information they receive through the filter of their beliefs. If someone is an atheist that person will interpret data differently than a Christian or a pantheist. If someone believes God created the world, that person's view of the world will be affected by that belief.

THE CLOSE

It's beyond the scope of this TalkSheet to discuss the details of the theories of evolution and creation. You may want to debate the relevance of creation versus evolution. However, the point that needs to be made is that God is involved in creation—in its beginning, sustenance, and end. He still is creating today—new people, plants, animals, and more! Scientists are still learning new things about the earth and the species on it.

You may want to point out the awesomeness of God's creation. What have your kids experienced that has put them at awe? A sunset? A sunrise? A new baby brother or sister? You may want to close by reading Psalm 100.

MORE

● If you have someone available, you may want to invite a science teacher, professor, or researcher to come into your meeting for discussion. Allow your students to ask questions, but encourage them also to listen carefully. Be careful to mediate the Q&A.

● Ask each of your kids to find two facts either for evolution or creation. Encourage them to search the Internet, check out their science textbooks at school, or ask their teacher. What information did they find? How does this information compare with the biblical account of creation? How have their beliefs been shaped from this discussion?

TOO MUCH, TOO SOON

1. What are three words (including the slang words) you know that describe or mean the same thing as **sex**?

2. Why do you think a sexually active guy is considered a **stud**, but a sexually active girl is seen as a **slut**?

3. Where do you stand with your friends?
   My friends are—
   ❑ More conservative about sex than I am
   ❑ Less conservative about sex than I am
   ❑ About the same as I am

4. In your opinion, are these statements **T (true)** or **N (not)**?
   ___ You're looked down at if you're a virgin.
   ___ Everyone assumes that if you're dating, then you're having sex.
   ___ You're expected to have sex with your date on prom night.
   ___ Teenagers are influenced to have sex by their peers and friends.
   ___ Most teenagers can get condoms and birth control easily from the school.
   ___ Teenagers abuse sex more than adults.
   ___ Sex is as normal and common as watching TV.
   ___ The athletes in school have sex more than other people.
   ___ Christian kids are assumed to be sexual prudes.
   ___ Teenagers should have access to birth control without parental permission.
   ___ Premarital sex can bring a relationship closer together.
   ___ STDs and pregnancy risks are keeping kids from having sex.
   ___ What the Bible says about sex doesn't matter today.
   ___ Sex is okay as long as both partners agree.
   ___ There's too much sexual temptation in the world.

5. How helpful has sex education at school been for you?

   Were your teachers honest when teaching you about sex?

   Why or why not?

6. Read the verses below and describe the sexual attitude and behavior in each one.
   Job 31:1   Proverbs 6:27-29
   Proverbs 5:18, 19   Titus 2:11-14

TOO MUCH TOO SOON [premarital sex]

THIS WEEK

Teenagers today are bombarded with the message that premarital sex is acceptable. Because the media, peers, and teachers tell them that it's okay, they need to hear the other side of the story in a positive, nonjudgmental way. This TalkSheet discusses sexuality in a Christian context. Be sensitive to your group members during this discussion. Some of your group member may be—or know someone who is—sexually active. Your goal is to let them know God's views of sex and not lay a guilt trip on your kids.

OPENER

Some people are reluctant to look at a road map when traveling, because they believe that they know where they are going. What are the attitudes of people who don't want to refer to maps to guide their travel? Tell the group that many people act the same way when it comes to sex. They have created a do-what-seems-right manual as their guide, instead of referring to God's Word to seek direction. Explain that you would like to talk about some of the attitudes and behaviors that young people have toward sex and take a look at the map God provided.

THE DISCUSSION, BY NUMBERS

1. What words has your group heard or learned that describe sex? Be careful—you may get some potentially offensive slang words. Why have people used these words to describe sex? If sex was created by God—a beautiful thing, for pleasure—why has society desecrated it?

2. The double standard persists—promiscuity is acceptable for males, but not females. Why is this the case? Are these attitudes present in your kids' schools?

3. Peers and friends influence teenagers more than any other group. Are your kids on the same track with their friends? Do their morals and values agree or disagree? What may happen if the two don't have the same views of sex?

4. Does your group agree with these statements? What is going on in their schools? Take some time to talk about these and how they affect their school experiences. They'll will probably generate a variety of responses. Let your kids debate the different issues that come up if you have time.

5. Discuss the pros and cons of school-based sex education. Most of your kids will have most likely gone through several sex ed classes by the time they reach the high school level.

6. Summarize the sexual attitudes and behaviors communicated in each of the passages. Point out how society has warped the meaning of sex in a number of ways. TV shows, movies, Internet pornographic sites, and other media have given the wrong messages about sex.

THE CLOSE

For sexual lives to be the best, Christians need to follow God's sexual directions given to us in the Bible. Make it very clear that God forgives any sin—even sexual sins—and he is listening to anyone who comes to him. You may wish to read a few verses about God's forgiveness and compassion—Isaiah 1:18 or 1 John 1:9. Encourage your kids to get right with God and to ask them for his self-control (a fruit of the Holy Spirit), wisdom, and strength to say no.

Let your group know that you are willing talk to them about sexual topics privately. According to the statistics, some of your kids have dealt with rape, sexual abuse, or abortion. Communicate with your kids that under no circumstances should anyone sexually abuse or rape another person. Both rape and sexual abuse are crimes, punished by years in prison (or worse). If your kids are victims of inappropriate comments, touches, or sexual aggression—or suspect others are—they must get help immediately from a school counselor, parent, pastor, or you. For more information, visit the Rape, Abuse, and Incest National Network (www.rainn.org) or National Coalition Against Sexual Assault (http://ncasa.org).

You may want to close by reading 1 Thessalonians 4:1-8 and a time of prayer for your kids to bring their concerns, fears, and hurts to God.

MORE

● Want to take this discussion on sexual behavior and attitudes further? Check out *Good Sex: A Whole-Person Approach to Teenage Sexuality & God* (Youth Specialties). This curriculum includes video segments for discussion and interactive student journals. For more information, visit www.YouthSpecialties.com.

● You may want to talk about abstinence with your group. If you feel your group is interested or ready, end with a challenge to commit to abstinence. How can your kids promote abstinence among themselves? For information, check out Aim for Success (www.aim-for-success.org), True Love Waits (www.truelovewaits.com), or the Youth Specialties Web page (www.YouthSpecialties.com) for links to information and resources.

IT'S YOUR CALL

1. In your own words, describe what **being responsible** means.

2. Teenagers shouldn't have to be as responsible as adults.
   - ❏ True for all areas of teenage life.
   - ❏ True for most areas of teenage life.
   - ❏ True for some areas of teenage life.
   - ❏ Not true at all.

3. Underline the **top three excuses** teenagers usually give for their irresponsibility.

   I'm too young.
   I'm not the one to blame.
   I forgot.
   I was mad.
   I didn't have enough time.
   I didn't know any better.
   I'm lazy.

   I couldn't control myself.
   I always have bad luck.
   I've never learned to be responsible.
   I'm not the one in charge.
   It doesn't matter to me.
   I think being responsible is boring.
   I don't feel like I can be responsible.

4. On a scale of 1-5 (1 being "I have absolutely no responsibility at all" and 5 being "I have a lot of responsibility"), how would you rate yourself?

   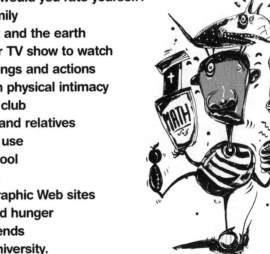

   ___ Getting along with your family
   ___ Caring for the environment and the earth
   ___ Discerning which movies or TV show to watch
   ___ Dealing with your own feelings and actions
   ___ Deciding how far to go with physical intimacy
   ___ Making the sports team or club
   ___ Witnessing to your friends and relatives
   ___ Controlling alcohol or drug use
   ___ Making good grades in school
   ___ Getting a date to the prom
   ___ Staying away from pornographic Web sites
   ___ Facing the problem of world hunger
   ___ Choosing your group of friends
   ___ Getting into a college or university.

5. Do you **agree** or **disagree** with this statement?
   If young people were given more control over their lives, they would be more responsible.

6. Check out the verses below and write down the responsibility given to Christians in each verse. How well are you doing in each of these areas?

   Genesis 1:28
   Matthew 25:14-30

   Matthew 27:24
   I Corinthians 15:33

   Philippians 1:27
   Romans 14:12

From *More High School TalkSheets—Updated!* by David Lynn. Permission to reproduce this page granted only for use in the buyer's own youth group. www.YouthSpecialties.com

IT'S YOUR CALL [responsibility]

THIS WEEK

Responsibility—teenagers say they can handle it. Adults question what teenagers do with it. How much responsibility is good for high schoolers and why? And how do your kids handle it? Use this TalkSheet opportunity to talk about this topic that is so important to maturity.

OPENER

You may want to start off by making a three-column master list of all the responsibilities that the kids in your group have. This may be a long list, depending on your group. Some responsibilities include homework, personal hygiene, babysitting, helping out around the house, getting to and from school safely, being honest with their parents, etc. On a scale of 1 to 10 (ten being very responsible), how would your kids rate themselves for each responsibility? In the second column record how their parents would rate them for each responsibility. Finally, in a third column record how they think God would rate them for each responsibility.

List some responsibilities that your kids will have as they get older. What role do their parents, teachers, or other adults have in the amount of responsibility that your kids have?

THE DISCUSSION, BY NUMBERS

1. Decide on a group definition of responsibility. Young people may define it as doing what they have to do, doing God's will, getting stuff done, meeting their obligations, being accountable for what they do, or doing their duties.

2. Young people want to be treated as if they are adults—but they don't always want adult responsibility. And they want to decide when they get to be responsible and when they get to be irresponsible. How can your kids be responsible and respect their parents at the same time?

3. Which of these excuses have your kids heard? You may want to talk about why so many people—not just teenagers—act irresponsibly. How does this hurt relationships with parents and friends? How can being irresponsible impact the future?

4. Ask the students to decide what their choices imply. How responsible are they really? What responsibility have their parents and God given them?

5. Teenagers' willingness to take responsibility reflects control over their lives. Which makes it interesting that young people are asked to take on more responsibility, but they aren't given control over the decisions that must be made in relation to the responsibility.

6. Maybe some of your kids will want to share how they're doing with regard to the responsibilities examined in the Bible verses. Are your kids on track with God?

THE CLOSE

Point out that the human nature is sinful—people like to blame others rather than taking responsibility. The "it's not my fault" thinking began in the garden with Adam and Eve—and it continues today! How can your kids balance their responsibilities with the view of their parents? Teachers? Coaches? Other adults?

Adults are concerned about irresponsibility because they're concerned about their teenagers. But teenagers see responsibility differently than adults. Most teenagers think they are acting responsibly with respect to their future—their "future" being tomorrow or tonight. Teenagers also think that responsibility is equal to growing up, but they've confused responsibility with maturity.

Close by pointing out that responsibility is a privilege—if your kids abuse their responsibilities, they'll most likely be punished somehow, either by parents, teachers, police, etc. Challenge your kids to honor their responsibilities and to start making wise choices for the future.

MORE

● You may want to ask parents, pastor, and some other adults to attend a panel for a Q & A with your students. Encourage your kids to ask questions and vice versa—how do adults know how much responsibility? How is trust involved in responsibility? What are the consequences for not being responsible? If you don't want to do a panel, encourage your kids to ask three adults questions on responsibility this week—challenge them to ask their teachers, coaches, parents, employers, and anyone else who hold them responsible.

● Give your kids responsibility and see how they follow through! A few suggestions include putting your kids in charge of next week's meeting, having them work together to plan an event or fundraiser, helping out the pastor plan a church service, etc. But don't make this a burden to your kids either! You can make this as fun as you want. And you can either do this before the meeting or after it—then talk about the responsibility later. How did they feel having these responsibilities? What did they like about it? What didn't they like? How do responsibilities now prepare them for future responsibilities?

DOWN AND OUT

1. Check the following events or feelings you've experienced within the last year. Then go back—did any of these make you feel absolutely down or depressed?

   ❏ Arguing with a parent about rules
   ❏ Feeling far away from God
   ❏ Missing church or church-related activities
   ❏ Breaking up with a boyfriend or girlfriend
   ❏ Arguing with a friend
   ❏ Transferring to a different school
   ❏ Being bigger or smaller than most people your age
   ❏ Being bored
   ❏ Having a conflict with your teacher
   ❏ Watching parents separate or divorce
   ❏ Having to turn in homework late
   ❏ Seeing your parents fight in front of you
   ❏ Fighting with a parent
   ❏ Getting a bad grade on a test
   ❏ Feeling left out of the youth group

   ❏ Being grounded or restricted
   ❏ Feeling underweight or overweight
   ❏ Feeling frustrated with your Christian life
   ❏ Having no time with one or both of your parents
   ❏ Being pressured to do something you know is wrong
   ❏ Moving to a new place
   ❏ Having to dress in a way you don't like, just to please others
   ❏ Arriving late for school or a class
   ❏ Trying out for a sport and not making the team or having to be on the bench
   ❏ Feeling rejected by a group of people your age
   ❏ Feeling pressured to succeed
   ❏ Getting a bad report card
   ❏ Being nagged by a parent

2. What do you think—**T (true)** or **F (false)**?
   ___ I feel down more than most people my age.
   ___ Depression can be treated with medications and counseling.
   ___ Circumstances can cause someone to become depressed.
   ___ Depression isn't really that serious.
   ___ People who are depressed use it as a cop-out.
   ___ Only old people deal with depression.
   ___ If I cry a lot or am moody, I may be depressed.
   ___ Depression is an actual disease—of the emotions.
   ___ Both adults and kids suffer from depression.
   ___ Only women suffer from depression.
   ___ Depression can lead to suicide.

3. When I feel down, I usually—

4. Check out these verses below—what does each one say about **depression**?
   Matthew 11:28-30
   2 Corinthians 1:8-11
   2 Corinthians 1:3-6
   Hebrews 10:23-25

From *More High School TalkSheets—Updated!* by David Lynn. Permission to reproduce this page granted only for use in the buyer's own youth group. www.YouthSpecialties.com

DOWN AND OUT [depression]

THIS WEEK

This TalkSheet provides a discussion for depression, what your kids think of depression, how to handle feeling down, and how to know if they need to get help to deal with their feelings. Before you start, it's crucial to know the facts about depression. Depression is a clinically diagnosed disease that affects millions of adults and teenagers each year. It's different than just having a bad day or feeling bad after a failed test. Be sensitive to your group members during this discussion and use this as an educational tool for them. And be sure to get the information you need before you start by checking out these Web sites—

- National Foundation For Depressive Illness, Inc. (www.depression.org)
- Depression Central(www.psycom.net/depression.central.html)
- Psychology Information Online (www.psychologyinfo.com/depression/index.html)
- Depression.com (www.depression.com)
- Disorders and Treatments (http://depression.mentalhelp.net)

Or consider talking with a psychologist or doctor about depression and it's affects.

OPENER

For a brief opener to this discussion, ask your kids what they think depression is. Some of them may have different ideas or misconceptions from the media. Make a master list of their ideas and words they use to describe depression. Now ask them this question—how many kids their age suffer from depression? Have them take a guesses at it. Then write down or read these facts to your group —

- Approximately 4 out of 100 teenagers get seriously depressed each year.
- Up to 20% of teenagers are diagnosed with some kind of mood disorder
- Depression can lead to suicide—the fifth leading cause of death among kids ages 5-14.

How does this information make your kids feel? Did they realize this information before? What does this information say about youth today and dealing with emotions and feelings?

THE DISCUSSION, BY NUMBERS

1. Let kids share the life events that have happened to them over the past six months. Point out that some of these events naturally cause people to feel down—and can trigger depression. How do your kids deal with these big changes? What are good and bad ways to deal with these changes?

2. This question will give you a feel for what your kids know or understand about depression. Some may not know or understand what it is. The facts are true—anyone, males and females, of any age can suffer from depression. It is more than feeling sad a lot, it's feeling down all the time—and it affects how a person's schoolwork, friendships, and physical health.

3. Create a master list of all the things that your group members do when they feel down. Split the list into healthy and unhealthy responses. What is the best solution for dealing with feeling down?

4. Ask for volunteers to read these verses and try to apply them to today. What do these verses say about depression and feeling down?

THE CLOSE

Encourage your kids to listen to their friends when they experience low points of life. Both Elijah and Job had friends who supported them when they were down (1 Kings 19:19-21; Job 2:11-13). It's important that your kids find someone to talk with and sort out their life situations that get them down.

Sometimes, feeling down turns into something more serious—clinical depression. These feelings of helplessness are powerful emotions that destroy lives, weaken relationships, and even lead to suicide (see links below)—and they don't go away with extra sleep or exercise. Communicate that if any of your kids, their family members, or friends are dealing with feelings of depression, they must find professional help. Encourage them to talk with a trusted adult to find help.

MORE

- You may want to talk about suicide with your group. What are some signs that your kids can look for in their friends or family members? Visit a few on-line organizations for more information—Suicide Voices Awareness of Education (www.save.org) and the American Foundation for Suicide Prevention (www.afsp.org). If there is a suicide hotline in your area, post the number for the kids to write down. You might also suggest the names of adult counselors in your area who are qualified to provide help to potential suicide victims.

- Ask your kids pay attention to what they hear or see in the media on depression and suicide. Possibly show a short clip of a TV show of a teenage problem and discuss ways to handle the problem. How does the media portray suicide and depression? What TV shows or movies have they seen that addresses these issues?

ECO-CHRISTIANS

1. Circle the one environmental issue listed below that you are most familiar with.

   Rainforest destruction   Species extinction
   Air pollution   Greenhouse effect
   Acid rain   Hazardous waste
   Ozone depletion   Garbage overload
   Water pollution   Natural resource depletion

2. Which of the following do you (or your family) do?
   - ❑ Recycle newspapers
   - ❑ Recycle paper and cardboard
   - ❑ Conserve the amount of water you use
   - ❑ Recycle soda cans and bottles
   - ❑ Throw away pretty much everything
   - ❑ Use a water-saving fixture in the shower
   - ❑ Recycle plastic bottles and containers
   - ❑ Get the car checked for smog and emissions
   - ❑ Reuse plastic cups and silverware
   - ❑ Carpool with others to save gas
   - ❑ Buy paper cups instead of styrofoam
   - ❑ Use a garbage disposal in your kitchen

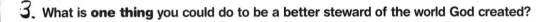

3. What is **one thing** you could do to be a better steward of the world God created?

   What could your **church** do?

   Your **family**?

   Your **school**?

4. If God were to take you to court, would you be found **innocent** or **guilty** of crimes against his creation?
   - ❑ Guilty as charged—I deserve a heavy sentence.
   - ❑ Guilty, but I'm a first-time offender.
   - ❑ Innocent.
   - ❑ Innocent by reason of insanity—I didn't know any better.

5. Check out these verses and paraphrase each one briefly in your own words.
   Genesis 1:27-30
   Psalm 8
   Romans 8:18-25
   1 Corinthians 10:26

From *More High School TalkSheets—Updated!* by David Lynn. Permission to reproduce this page granted only for use in the buyer's own youth group. www.YouthSpecialties.com

ECO-CHRISTIANS [the environment]

THIS WEEK

There's a lot of emphasis today on environmental issues. Various New Age-influenced groups have used these environmental issues to spread their messages. But most young people in the church have little concept of a Christian view of ecology. Christians—those who love God—should care for God's world, too! Take this opportunity to talk about a Christian perspective of the environment.

OPENER

You may want to open by giving your group some statistics about the condition of the earth. For more information on the environment, current problems, and solutions, check out OECD Environment (www.oecd.org/env), Friends of the Earth (www.foe.org), Greenpeace (www.greenpeace.org), or Resources for the Future (www.rff.org). You'll be able to find some stories or other information to share with the group as well.

Or you could test the responsibility of your group. Before the meeting, litter your meeting area with some crumpled papers, empty soda cans, dry cups, and some other (safe) garbage. As your kids walk in, check to see if they pick it up or not. Use this litter as an illustration for the TalkSheet—did your kids feel like they should've picked it up? Why or why not?

THE DISCUSSION, BY NUMBERS

1. Do your kids know what these problems are? What are the three most important issues today? What are the most threatening ones for our world?

2. Which of these do your kids or their families do? Take a poll from the whole group to see which ones are done the most. Why are some easier than others? What difference does each one make?

3. What can your kids do to be stewards of the earth? What about the church? Schools? Brainstorm a list of ideas and have them decide what to do from this list—could they get things going in the church or school? Could your group start a recycling program? What else could they do?

4. How would your group members do? You may want to take a poll to see if they would be guilty or not and why. How about their peers in general? How about society at large?

5. God has given Christians an awesome responsibility to take care of his creation. How does your group think God feels about the kind of job Christians have been doing taking care of his creation?

THE CLOSE

Most New Age philosophies seek to elevate the animal, plant, and mineral world to the level of human beings. They see all things as an undifferentiated oneness, a worldview called monism—that leads to the pantheistic view that all is one, all is god. And because all is divine, all should be treated equally. In contrast to this, the Bible teaches that people are created in God's image (Genesis 1:26). People are uniquely divided from the animal, plant, and mineral world.

Yet, people are united with that world because all of it was created by God and all of it has value (Leviticus 25:23; 1 Chronicles 29:14-16; Psalm 50:10, 11; and Haggai 2:8). It is this Christian view of creation that gives creation its purpose. God created animals, plants, oceans, and mountains—and they are worth respecting. People are responsible for creation because God created man above everything else. Christians have a responsibility to be good stewards of the earth. But sin has affected creation—people have exploited and abused the earth. But the Bible teaches that the whole of creation awaits God's redemption (Romans 8:18-25). God will fix all of creation when he returns. In the meantime, he's put people—Christians included—in charge of taking care of the world.

MORE

● To tie the lesson in with your group, you may want to have some of your group members take turns recycling the trash, soda cans and bottles, and paper cups accumulated at youth group events. Some states give refunds for soda cans and bottles. You may want to encourage your congregation to bring their recyclable materials to church for the youth group to recycle and use as a fundraiser for your group.

● You may want to talk about the contradictions within society on pollution. Why is our society so concerned about the earth, but still wastes so much? What responsibilities to companies have to package their materials in biodegradable packaging? What about fast food restaurants or other companies? What responsibilities to schools or businesses have to recycle?

MASQUERADE

1. Check the **two words** that you think best describe hypocrisy.
   - ❑ Typical
   - ❑ Opposite
   - ❑ Self-righteous
   - ❑ Sinful
   - ❑ Rebellious
   - ❑ Two-faced
   - ❑ Necessary
   - ❑ Sad
   - ❑ Selfish
   - ❑ Smart
   - ❑ Intolerable
   - ❑ Fake

2. In your opinion—

   Do you think it's better to believe in Christ and not live the Christian life, or to not believe in Christ at all?

3. Do you think each of these statements is **T (true)** or **F (false)**?
   - ___ You have to be a hypocrite to survive in high school.
   - ___ Some people are bigger hypocrites than others.
   - ___ The church should lower its standards to avoid hypocrisy.
   - ___ Parents force their kids to be hypocritical.
   - ___ People are hypocrites because they worry about what others think of them.
   - ___ Christians are less hypocritical than other people.

4. How often do you live what you believe?
   - ❑ Every day
   - ❑ Most every day
   - ❑ Some days
   - ❑ Sundays
   - ❑ No days

5. How would you finish this sentence?

   The reason Christian young people act like hypocrites is—
   - ❑ They cave into peer pressure.
   - ❑ That's the way teenagers are.
   - ❑ They are forced to be hypocrites by their parents.
   - ❑ They know what they are doing is wrong but they do it anyway.
   - ❑ They don't know any better.
   - ❑ They're are just being rebellious.
   - ❑ Other—

6. Read each of the following verses and circle the one that comes closest to describing your life.

   Matthew 23:28
   Romans 7:15-20

   Galatians 5:19-21
   Ephesians 4:22-24

   Philippians 2:12, 13
   1 Thessalonians 5:22

From *More High School TalkSheets—Updated!* by David Lynn. Permission to reproduce this page granted only for use in the buyer's own youth group. www.YouthSpecialties.com

MASQUERADE [personal hypocrisy]

THIS WEEK

Do your kids practice what they preach? This TalkSheet will give you an opportunity to talk about hypocrisy with your kids. You'll need to be sensitive to the spiritual condition of the individuals in your group—some may be more into Christianity than others. Keep an open and honest discussion with your kids. And be careful not to be too judgmental or heavy-handed—your goal isn't to drive the kids into hypocrisy, but closer to the Lord.

OPENER

What's a masquerade? A masquerade is a costume dance where people dress up in full costumes and masks. If you don't want to have a full masquerade with your group, that's okay! Ask your group why people like masquerade dances and dressing up on Halloween. Why are so many pranks pulled on Halloween? Why do bank robbers and other criminals cover their faces with ski masks? Simple—they want to hide their identity! People want to get away with things they normally wouldn't do. They want to feel safe by hiding their faces. Hypocrisy is exactly like wearing a mask—people pretend to be someone that they're not, and they think they're getting away with something. What other "masks" do high schoolers put on? How do kids their age keep others from seeing who they really are?

THE DISCUSSION, BY NUMBERS

1. Make a master list of the words that your students checked. Include additional words they considered while doing the activity. You will likely discover that personal hypocrisy is a major problem for Christian teenagers.

2. This will most likely prove to be a controversial question. Let your kids debate their opinions. You may want to split the group up into two sides to argue this question.

3. How did your kids respond to these statements? Take a few minutes to talk about them. How true are these statements for the kids at their school?

4. Point out that hypocrisy is a survival skill. How much of a reality is this for the members of your group? What are other alternatives to hypocrisy for surviving in high school? How do Christians compare to other people? How is it for your kids to be Christians in their own schools?

5. This question forces your kids to examine how consistently they practice what they preach. If you don't want to ask for individual answers, ask your kids how often Christian kids their age practice

what they preach? How about non-Christian kids? Their teachers? Parents? Pastors?

6. These passages describe various degrees of spiritual commitment or lack of it. Ask for volunteers to share where they see themselves. Your group should provide a degree of safety for those who are far from God to honestly share.

THE CLOSE

One way to look at hypocrisy is to view it as the opposite of repentance. Instead of realizing a sin and confessing it, a hypocrite pretends to ignore the problem. The hypocrite goes through the Christian motions for the purpose of fooling others or perhaps himself or herself. Young people need to realize that everyone is hypocritical to some extent. People are hypocrites every time they judge one another (Matthew 7:1) and are hypocrites every time they talk about their sin in the past tense (1 John 1:8). The Bible warns against being deceived by sin, which causes hypocrisy (Jeremiah 17:9; Romans 7:11; and 1 Corinthians 3:18).

What can your kids do to be less hypocritical? How can a stronger relationship with God help them and others be less hypocritical? What can your kids do today to get right with God and others? Close with a time of prayer with your group.

MORE

● Where have your kids seen hypocrisy in society in the past few months or year? Has their been a celebrity or other famous person that has been hypocritical—and gotten caught? Be careful not to put judgment on these people—instead, ask your group what ramifications may come with being hypocritical. Do celebrities and other famous people have more responsibility than others? Why or why not? How does fame or popularity affect how people act? How about Christians who are in these situations? Do they have a greater responsibility?

● How does hypocrisy compare to lying? What do your kids think is worse—having a friend lie to them or act hypocritical toward them? How do they handle it if a friend lies to them? Cheats on them? Or just acts like two different people? What happens to the friendship or relationship? How does it change and why? How does hypocrisy relate to trusting and respecting others?

MISSION IMPOSSIBLE?

1. When can you first remember wondering about the opposite sex?
   - ❑ Before elementary school (Pre-k to kindergarten)
   - ❑ Early elementary school (grades 1-4)
   - ❑ Later elementary school (grades 5-6)
   - ❑ Junior high
   - ❑ High school

2. What **one word** do you think best describes the opposite sex?

3. Below are a few statements about girls and guys in relationships. Put a **F** by the ones you feel apply more to **girls/females** and an **M** by those that apply more to **guys/males**.

   ___ Cheating in a relationship
   ___ Pressuring to get more physical
   ___ Preferring to spend time with friends
   ___ Being possessive
   ___ Having higher standards
   ___ Being sensitive
   ___ Being competitive
   ___ Being jealous

   ___ Being domineering
   ___ Wanting to get serious
   ___ Being committed to God
   ___ Leading the other person on
   ___ Being romantic
   ___ Being demanding
   ___ Being argumentative

4. What do you think?
   Can girls and guys be friends without getting romantically involved with each other?
   - ❑ Nope—it's too hard
   - ❑ Could happen, but it's not likely
   - ❑ Probably could happen, depending on both people
   - ❑ Definitely—sometimes those are the best friendships to have

5. If you could ask all members of the opposite sex one question, what would it be?

6. Check out these verses from Ephesians. What does each have to say about relating to the opposite sex?

   Ephesians 4:2
   Ephesians 4:25
   Ephesians 4:29

   Ephesians 4:32
   Ephesians 5:1
   Ephesians 6:18

From *More High School TalkSheets—Updated!* by David Lynn. Permission to reproduce this page granted only for use in the buyer's own youth group. www.YouthSpecialties.com

MISSION IMPOSSIBLE? [relating to the opposite sex]

THIS WEEK

The battle of the sexes rages on, but need this be the case for Christians? Maybe so, but you can help bridge the gap with this TalkSheet designed to help Christian young men and women better relate to each other. As teenagers progress through the adolescent years, they learn to develop mature relationships with the opposite sex. (See also Too Much Too Soon, page 69).

OPENER

Illustrate the differences in thinking among girls and guys. Call two volunteers—a guy and a girl—to the front of the group. Let the girl leave the room, and read the situation to the guy in front of the group. Let the group note how the guy answered or reacted to the situation. Now let the girl in and read her the same situation. How did she react? Ask the group the differences they noticed between how each answered. What does this say about girl versus guy communication? Need a few situations to get started? How about these—

- You've just got cut from the swim (or whatever) team and your best friends made it. How do you react?
- You've just gotten a low (almost failing) on the hardest exam you've ever taken. How are you feeling?
- You just found out that there is a girl (or guy) that likes you. What will you do about it?
- Your sister or brother hits you hard—and I mean hard. What are you going to do?
- Your mom and dad are splitting up—for good. What will you tell your friends?
- A kid in the hallway calls you a name. What are you going to do about it?

THE DISCUSSION, BY NUMBERS

1. This should prime the memories of your group and generate a variety of stories. Be prepared to share your memories as well!

2. Make a master list of the words that your kids chose and why. Keep the list of questions running throughout the discussion and have the group answer them at the end of the session..

3. Wow! The discussion sparks will fly when you look at these. Examine the differences and similarities between the sexes. Decide how many are cultural and how many are God-given.

4. This has always been a topic of discussion between young men and women. Discuss what kinds of friendships Christian young men and women can have and how these can be developed.

5. What questions do your kids have? Keep a list of these questions and take some time to answer them. You may want to have your adult leaders help you answer these, as well as other kids in your group.

6. What did these verses say about relating to the opposite sex? What different interpretations did the males and females have?

THE CLOSE

Because young women and men have so many questions and concerns about the opposite sex, you'll probably have covered a lot in your discussion. Emphasize that there are both differences and similarities between the sexes—focus on the "one another" passages found in Ephesians, and challenge your young people to have friendship relationships with the opposite sex that aren't romantically based. You may also want to illustrate the friendship between Jesus and Mary Magdalene (Luke 8:2 and John 20), and Mary and Martha (Luke 10:38-42). Jesus had close relationships with women in the Bible—yet was never romantically involved with them. How can your kids reflect the love of Jesus in their relationships with the opposite sex?

Close with a time of prayer with your group and give your kids time to pray for their friends and relationships.

MORE

- What does the media say about girl and guy relationships? How often do friends in movies or TV shows land up in dating relationships? Can this transition ruin friendships? Why or why not? You may want to ask your kids what TV shows or movies they've seen where friendships turn into romantic relationships. What happened?
- You may want to ask a panel of people—including parents, college students, and some grandparents—for a Q&A session with your group. Encourage your kids to ask questions about how to relate to the opposite sex. How do relationships and friendships change in high school and in college? How can girls and guys get to be better friends? How are friendships and dating situations different?

WALKING WITH GOD

1. How often do you think about each of the following? **A (all the time)**, **S (sometimes)**, or **N (never)?**
   ___ Wanting a closer relationship with God
   ___ Wishing you could actually see God
   ___ Wondering if and when God is listening to your prayers
   ___ Feeling that something is missing in your relationship with God
   ___ Considering questions about God and Christianity that don't seem to have any real answers
   ___ Wondering if all this Christian stuff is a waste of time
   ___ Wishing you could understand God

2. What do you think—**Y (yes)** or **N (no)?**
   ___ If you know about God, you know God.
   ___ You should feel closest to God at church.
   ___ Getting to know God is quite difficult.
   ___ Pastors (or those in ministry) feel closer to God than others.
   ___ There's no one right way to grow in a relation ship with God.
   ___ If Christ had not become a human being, we could not have a personal relationship with God.

3. Suppose you were one of Jesus' 12 disciples.
   Do you think that as one of the disciples, you could have known God more personally than you do now? Why or why not?

4. Think about your relationship with God and answer these questions—

   How is your relationship with God **like a friendship**?

   How is your relationship with God **unlike a friendship**?

5. What does each of these verses say about personally relating with God?
   Psalm 84:2   Colossians 1:21-23
   Psalm 89:46   Hebrews 2:14
   Isaiah 6:3-7   Hebrews 4:14-16
   John 1:18

WALKING WITH GOD [knowing God]

THIS WEEK

Young people want to know God—not know *about* God, but *know* God. They want a personal relationship with him. They want to see him, talk with him, and walk with him. Take this opportunity to discuss personal, intimate relationships with God.

OPENER

What makes things grow? What does a person have to do to get things growing? What about a baby? A child? A plant? An animal? Other things in the world? Why do some take more effort to grow than others? Why is it harder to grow certain kinds of plants than others? Why do some kids grow faster than other kids? Brainstorm about these questions with your group.

Now compare this to a person's spiritual growth. What do people have to do to grow spiritually? Do your kids think it takes work or not? What happens if they don't get "fed"? Point out that not everyone grows at the same rate or in the same way. How do some Christians grow in Christ differently than others? Why are some people deeper spiritually than others?

THE DISCUSSION, BY NUMBERS

1. Let volunteers share their doubts or interests in a relationship with God. Point out that the psalmist felt the same way (Psalm 42).

2. Let your kids talk about and debate each of these statements. Point out to the group that knowing God isn't as easy or as hard as they make it out to be. God is as close to them as their next prayer.

3. What may have been different about this time in history? What would it have been like being close friends with Christ? Is this different from your relationship with him today? You may want to illustrate this by reading Matthew 28:17.

4. You won't find the phrase "personal relationship with Jesus Christ" in the Bible. But God does tell us in other ways that he wants to be close to Christians. What insight do your kids have about how a relationship with God is like and unlike a friendship?

5. What did your kids learn from these passages? You may want to create a master list to record the insights of the group.

THE CLOSE

Point out to the group that the metaphor of walking with God is a useful way to look at how we relate to him. There are different ways we walk with people. For example, if you go to the mall with your parents, you might walk away from them—you don't want your friends to see you so close to them. When walking with a boyfriend or a girlfriend, you might hold hands or walk arm in arm. If you have the unfortunate experience of walking with a police officer who has taken you into custody—you might walk with your head lowered! On the other hand, you might walk casually and coolly with your friends. Ask the kids to describe how they are walking with God. Does their walk change from day to day? Why or why not?

There's a bumper sticker that reads "If you don't feel close to God, guess who moved." Point out to you kids that God never moves from them—they move away from God. Encourage your kids to get closer with God by drawing near to him. James 4:8 says "Come near to God and he will come near to you." Read this verse and spend some time in prayer, giving your kids time to think about God and draw near to him.

MORE

● Encourage those in your group who are interested to keep spiritual journals of their walk with God for one week. Mention that journaling is useful to write thoughts, prayer requests, and ideas of God down on paper. Suggest time to journal—while reading the Bible, listening to music, during prayer, or while thinking about your day. You may want to talk about their experiences—what did they learn by journaling? Did it help their walk with God or not? If so, how?

● What gets in the way of your kids' relationship with God? Do they not have enough time? Are they too tired at night to talk with God? Challenge your kids to set aside a few minutes a day to spend with God. It doesn't even have to be very long—just a goal to make time for God. After all, friends should spend time together, right?

WHITE LIES AND OTHER HALF-TRUTHS

1. People seem to divide lies into two categories—**white lies** and **real lies**. Give an example of what the average person would classify as "white lie" and "real lie."

2. Would you consider this to be absolutely **true** or **false**?
There are times when you have no choice but to lie.

3. Which of these (if any) would justify telling a lie?
   - ❑ To get you out of trouble
   - ❑ To sharpen your lying skills
   - ❑ To protect a friend
   - ❑ To cover up a mistake
   - ❑ To protect yourself from a stranger
   - ❑ To boost your self-image
   - ❑ To hide a past experience
   - ❑ To get your parents or family off your back
   - ❑ To avoid hurting another's feelings
   - ❑ To keep a secret
   - ❑ To get something for yourself
   - ❑ To save someone's life

4. What do you think of the following statement?
There's a difference between lying and not telling all of the truth.
   - ❑ They are absolutely different.
   - ❑ I agree, for the most part.
   - ❑ No, they're the same thing.
   - ❑ I would strongly disagree.
   - ❑ Don't ask me. I have no idea.

5. Think about the last time you deliberately lied.
   a. Was it easier to tell the lie than it would've been to tell the truth?
   b. What could you have done to avoid the lie?
   c. What happened because you lied?
   d. How comfortable did you feel telling the lie?
   e. Do you believe your own lies?

6. What is one lie you have told that you wish you could take back?

7. Pick one of the following Bible verses to rewrite in your own words.
   Psalm 5:6   Ephesians 4:25   Proverbs 19:9   Colossians 3:9

From *More High School TalkSheets—Updated!* by David Lynn. Permission to reproduce this page granted only for use in the buyer's own youth group. www.YouthSpecialties.com

83

WHITE LIES AND OTHER HALF-TRUTHS [lying]

THIS WEEK

Some teenagers tell the truth, others lie to escape painful consequences. Some say they have to lie, and others lie when it would be easier to tell the truth. Lying is a common strategy young people use to get through adolescence. God was clear in the Bible about the dangers of lying, yet young people often have difficulty seeing the consequences of deception. Use this TalkSheet to explore this often confusing issue.

OPENER

You may want to start by asking the group the following question—if you were to be hooked up to a lie detector, would you agree to answer any question your parents asked you? How about any question your youth pastor asked you? Your best friend? Your boyfriend or girlfriend? Why would some questions be harder to answer honestly than others? How do they feel knowing that God already knows all their answers!?

Or you may want to talk about ways that lying is considered good or bad. Make a master list of their ideas. For example, girls might think it's okay to lie to a strange man who is asking them personal questions. What are some other examples of situations? What would be other ways to handle these situations besides just lying? How does the media portray lying? Does it portray it as good or bad? Necessary? How has this altered the "black and white" of lying?

THE DISCUSSION, BY NUMBERS

1. Ask the group to clarify the difference between a little white lie and a real lie. Many people honestly believe that their lies are harmless, especially those little white lies that people feel are necessary for survival. The important (but often unasked) question is how do we know that our good intentions will in fact turn out good?

2. Teenagers think in the immediate, not in the past or the future. The here and now is where they live. So lying as a survival strategy appears effective in the present. Lying to parents and other authority figures to escape discipline is seen as an easy way out (or is it?). The Lord gave guidelines that work for the long haul in life. There are biblical examples of lying out of fear (Genesis 18:15), lying in order to avoid trouble (Matthew 28:13, 14), and lying to look religious (Acts 5:1, 2). None of these lies are acceptable to God.

3. Each of the reasons listed are perceived payoffs for lying. It's easy to confuse a payoff with a

justification for lying. Getting something out of it doesn't make it right.

4. What does your group think about this? Is telling only some of the truth is the same as lying? How about twisting the truth? How do your kids define lying?

5. Have different students volunteer to answer the questions. What consequences came from their lie, if any? How about the other questions?

6. Don't ask your kids to share their lies aloud. Instead ask them to reflect on what they learned from thinking about the lie they wish they never said. What damage was done by the lie?

7. Ask some of the group members to read their personalized versions of the Bible verses aloud. You may want to choose a couple to talk about with the group.

THE CLOSE

Point out that lying causes damage because it breaks trust. And those who lie—and get away with it—find it easier to lie than to tell the truth, especially in a sticky situation. It can be addictive.

God straight out says that lying is wrong. Take some time to talk about this with your kids in light of the opening activity. Remind them that God is faithful, and that he loves them and forgives them. Encourage them to get right with God and others who they've hurt by lying. And challenge them to make honesty their number one goal from now on.

MORE

● You may want to talk more about how lying affects trust and respect in relationships. How can lying hurt a friendship, a relationship with a boyfriend or girlfriend, or relationships with parents? What happens when someone is caught lying? What happens when someone lies to police, judges, or other officials? What does lying say about respecting oneself and others?

● How does lying relate to hypocrisy and living the Christian life? How does hypocrisy compare to lying? What do your kids think is worse—having a friend lie to them or act hypocritical toward them? How do they handle it if a friend lies to them? Cheats on them? Or just acts like two different people? What happens to the friendship or relationship? How does it change and why? How does hypocrisy relate to trusting and respecting others?

FRIENDS

1. What does it mean to be called a **friend**?

2. Why do some teenagers change their group of friends?
   - ❑ They simply need a change.
   - ❑ They have an alcohol or drug problem.
   - ❑ They broke up with a girlfriend or boyfriend.
   - ❑ They're changing their values.
   - ❑ They've joined a sports team or club.
   - ❑ They're trying to change their image.
   - ❑ They've changed religious beliefs.
   - ❑ They have a parent who wants them to make a change.
   - ❑ They aren't in the same crowd as the people they really like.
   - ❑ They were forced to change friends because of a move.
   - ❑ Other—

3. How many Christian friends should a Christian teenager have?
   - ❑ None. It's really not that important.
   - ❑ They should have a few Christian friends.
   - ❑ Most of their friends should be Christians.
   - ❑ Their closest friends should be Christians
   - ❑ All their friends should be Christians.

4. Do you think this statement is **true** or **false**?
   Teenagers are more likely to reveal stuff to their friends than to their parents.
   Why, do you think?

5. Read each of the following verses from Proverbs. What characteristic of **friendship** is described in each one?
   Proverbs 13:20
   Proverbs 17:17
   Proverbs 18:24
   Proverbs 27:17

From *More High School TalkSheets—Updated!* by David Lynn. Permission to reproduce this page granted only for use in the buyer's own youth group. www.YouthSpecialties.com

FRIENDS [friends]

THIS WEEK

Friends are the lifeblood of adolescence. And yet what teenager hasn't had problems with friends? Kids learn valuable lifelong lessons from friendships, grow in Christ through friends, get into trouble because of friends, and fall in love with friends. Obviously friends are important, so it is vital that you and your teens discuss their questions and concerns.

OPENER

The media teaches teenagers a lot about friendships. Ask your group to think of all the TV shows or movies where they've seen friendships—there will be a ton of these, since almost every TV show and movie revolves around friendships and relationships. Make a list of these shows and how friendship is portrayed. What have your kids learned about friendship from these shows? What makes these shows successful? What is the difference between opposite and same sex friendships? Why do the characters value each other as friends? How have these friendships been abused or damaged?

It might be helpful to brainstorm and write down all the words that would apply to friendship—love, respect, sense of humor, honesty, trust, and so on. Encourage the group to think about what is most important in their friendships and what they look for in their friends. Then share these with the group—what were the most important attributes of friends? What do your kids look for in friendships? Why are some qualities more valuable than others? What characteristics are important for different sexes?

THE DISCUSSION, BY NUMBERS

1. Make a list of everyone's contributions. Survey the list and ask the group how much commonality there is among the group's responses. What are different among the guys and girls?

2. Teenagers change friends frequently for a variety of reasons—some reasons are good, some aren't. Discuss how kids can know when they are making changes for the worse. Why do they think kids change friends?

3. Answers will vary greatly on this one, but stay away from lecturing kids about the importance of Christian influence. Rather, share your own positive experiences regarding support and direction from Christian friends.

4. Some parents are more understanding and approachable than others. But some kids don't have good relationships with their parents. Encourage them to have friends, but still keep in mind that their parents have good things to say, too.

5. Ask volunteers to read the passages and share the friendship characteristic taught. You may want to make a list of these.

THE CLOSE

Close by reviewing some of the "one another" passages found in God's Word.

- Love one another
  John 15:12, 13
  Romans 12:10
  Ephesians 5:1, 2
  Hebrews 13:1
  1 Peter 4:8

- Discipline one another
  Matthew 18:15
  Galatians 6:12
  Thessalonians 3:14, 15
  Hebrews 12:15

- Don't hold grudges toward one another
  Matthew 5:22
  Galatians 6:2

- Forgive one another
  Matthew 18:21, 22
  Ephesians 4:31, 32

- Pray for one another
  Ephesians 6:18, 19
  James 5:16

- Be patient with one another
  Ephesians 4:2

- Carry one another's burdens
  Romans 15:1
  James 5:16

- Serve one another
  Ephesians 5:21
  1 Peter 4:9, 10

- Worship with one another
  Psalm 95:6

MORE

● You may want to have your group take a look at biblical friendships. A few examples include David and Jonathan (1 Samuel 18 and 19), Jesus and Lazarus (John 11), Moses and God (Exodus 33), and Paul and Barnabas (Acts 14). What makes these friendships good? What qualities of friendship were shown? Are these still important today? Why or why not?

● You may want to talk about the important aspects of friendships. Point out that to have friends, you've got to be a friend. And emphasize healthy friendships vs. unhealthy friendships. Do their friends pressure them into doing drugs? Alcohol? Being sexually active? Challenge your kids to choose friends who build them up and encourage them to be their best—friendship is about supporting and caring for each other for who they are, not what they are. Jesus is an example of a loyal, loving friend. What can your kids do to be better friends to others and to be a better friend with God?

WWW.X-RATED.SIN

1. When you see a **warning sign** (something like "contains explicit sexual content") on an Internet site, what do you do?
   - ❏ See what kind of Web site it was first.
   - ❏ Check to see if there was an age restriction.
   - ❏ Immediately close the site.
   - ❏ Think it was a joke.
   - ❏ Ignore the warning—I can look at what I want.
   - ❏ Tell my parent or adult who checks the history of the Internet files
   - ❏ Lie when it asks for my age, agree to the conditions, and start surfing.

2. In a few words, what is your definition of **obscene**?

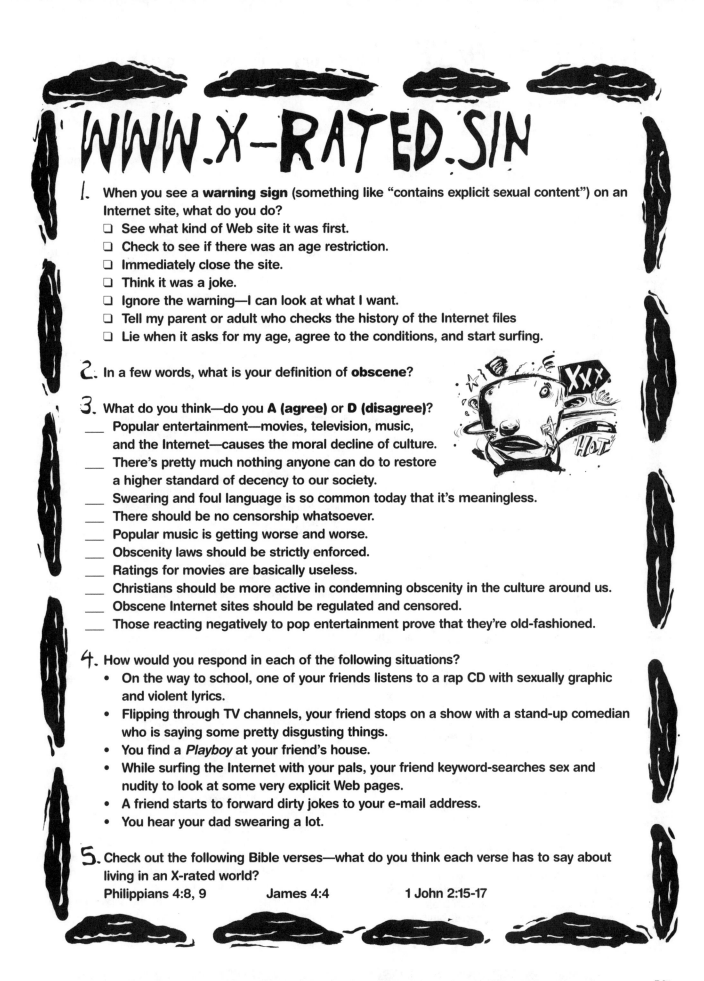

3. What do you think—do you **A (agree)** or **D (disagree)**?
   - ___ Popular entertainment—movies, television, music, and the Internet—causes the moral decline of culture.
   - ___ There's pretty much nothing anyone can do to restore a higher standard of decency to our society.
   - ___ Swearing and foul language is so common today that it's meaningless.
   - ___ There should be no censorship whatsoever.
   - ___ Popular music is getting worse and worse.
   - ___ Obscenity laws should be strictly enforced.
   - ___ Ratings for movies are basically useless.
   - ___ Christians should be more active in condemning obscenity in the culture around us.
   - ___ Obscene Internet sites should be regulated and censored.
   - ___ Those reacting negatively to pop entertainment prove that they're old-fashioned.

4. How would you respond in each of the following situations?
   - On the way to school, one of your friends listens to a rap CD with sexually graphic and violent lyrics.
   - Flipping through TV channels, your friend stops on a show with a stand-up comedian who is saying some pretty disgusting things.
   - You find a *Playboy* at your friend's house.
   - While surfing the Internet with your pals, your friend keyword-searches sex and nudity to look at some very explicit Web pages.
   - A friend starts to forward dirty jokes to your e-mail address.
   - You hear your dad swearing a lot.

5. Check out the following Bible verses—what do you think each verse has to say about living in an X-rated world?
   Philippians 4:8, 9   James 4:4   1 John 2:15-17

From
More High School TalkSheets—Updated! by David Lynn. Permission to reproduce this page granted only for use in the buyer's own youth group. www.YouthSpecialties.com

WWW.X-RATED.SIN [vulgarity and pornography]

THIS WEEK

Today's pop culture is crude and lewd and growing more profane with TV shows, musical groups, and blockbuster hits at the movies. Kids today aren't sheltered. This TalkSheet gives you the opportunity to talk with your kids about the affect that obscenity has on their lives. For more discussion on pornography, look at Smut World (pg. 103).

OPENER

You may want to ask the group for examples of obscenity in your community, in their lives, at their schools, or from the media. These answers will range from T-shirts with sexually explicit messages to TV programming. From their experiences, how easy is it to access pornographic material? Do they know of a sibling or friend who abuses pornography?

As you open this discussion, do be sensitive to these topics. Some of your kids may be involved with pornography, frequently watch obscenities, or more—you don't want to come off as too judgmental. Challenge the group to handle this discussion honestly and maturely. Be sure to mediate this discussion carefully. Some churches and youth are more open-minded than others.

THE DISCUSSION, BY NUMBERS

1. If they're honest, some will admit that they've seen objectionable material on the Web. Do they pay attention to the warning signs, if there are any? How would they handle this situation? Do they understand how easy it is to click on the mouse and find these materials?

2. Discuss the different definitions people have of obscenity. Many kids will mention sex in their definition. Make sure you point out that sex and obscenity are not the same. Read a dictionary definition of the word. Webster's New World Dictionary defines it as "offensive to modesty or decency; lewd."

3. Open these statements up to debate, especially if a difference of opinion exists. Several of the questions will promote discussion around the idea of how much society should tolerate. Expect the First Amendment question of freedom to be raised. Does it guarantee total freedom if society has the right to restrict certain things?

4. These tension-getters make great role-play situations as well as discussion starters on how to handle everyday situations involving the obscene. Ask the teens to share their own tension-getters that they have faced. The group can brainstorm Christian responses to these difficult but real dilemmas.

5. Discuss with the students how this verse applies to the pop culture that surrounds them. Why should Christians particularly keep their guard up against pornography?

THE CLOSE

Point out that standards of decency have eroded because society has allowed them to erode. The obscene no longer exists on the fringes of culture but has become the mainstream. But is that what Christians want? Is that what society wants? Culture will continue its decline as long as it's allowed.

Encourage your kids to get grounded in God. The way to avoid temptation is to ask for God's strength—it's the Holy Spirit that provides self-control and discernment. Close with a time of prayer and challenge your kids to ask God for strength and forgiveness.

MORE

● You may want to ask your group to think of an average young teenager—both a guy and a girl. What are some of the attitudes and behaviors of this average high schooler? What do they watch, listen to, or hear? Mention things that your kids have brought up during your discussion (things like viewing R-rated movies, reading dirty jokes, using vulgar language, and so on). How does getting hooked on vulgarity and pornography alter someone's life? Ask the group to predict the kind of life this person may live as they grow older—
  ⇨ What kind of relationship with God will they have?
  ⇨ What kind of parent will they be?
  ⇨ What kind of values will they adopt?
  ⇨ How will this person treat others?
  ⇨ How will they handle dating relationships?
  ⇨ What will they teach their kids about vulgarity and pornography?
● You may want to talk with your group about how to handle pornography. It is an addiction—in a sense, a visual drug. Teenage boys in particular struggle with these temptations. Discuss how easy it is to get hooked and what the dangers are. How does pornography affect their relationships? How they see the opposite sex? What they think of love and intercourse? Challenge your kids to seek out help if they or a friend are caught in a web of pornography. They must find another trusted person to talk with. For more information, check out Caught By the Web (www.caught-bytheweb.com), Focus on the Family's resources (www.pureintimacy.org), or Breaking Free From Pornography (www.porn-free.org). These are Christian links—if you search for pornography in a general search engine, you may land up with some not-so-helpful, unhealthy links!

THE BLURRING OF MORALITY

1. On a scale of **1-10** (**1** being **"breaking every one"** and **10** being **"keeping every one"**), how well do you think our society follows the Ten Commandments?

   How about the world at large?

2. When do you have the **hardest time** telling right from wrong?

   Why are some times harder than others?

3. What do you think—do you **A (agree)** or **D (disagree)**?

   ___ A decline in moral values is the number one problem facing the country.

   ___ Girls have better morals than guys.

   ___ There's a difference between what teens think of morality and what they're supposed to think.

   ___ People are more concerned about not getting caught than doing the right thing.

   ___ People have to decide for themselves what is right and what is wrong.

   ___ Most teenagers understand the difference between right and wrong.

4. If you had to talk to a fifth-grade class about morality, what would you say?

   How would you explain the difference between **right** and **wrong** (or black and white)?

5. Read each of the passages and complete the sentences.

   Ecclesiastes 7:20—No one can do right all the time because—

   Mark 10:31—Christ turns the world's values around by—

   Ephesians 2:1-5—Being dead in our sins means we should now—

   1 John 2:15-17—Christians need to reject the world's values because—

From *More High School TalkSheets—Updated!* by David Lynn. Permission to reproduce this page granted only for use in the buyer's own youth group. www.YouthSpecialties.com

THE BLURRING OF MORALITY [morality]

THIS WEEK

What's right and what's wrong has been distorted by society today. Teenagers have been left with varied and blurred concepts of morality. For this reason, parents and churches must be more intentional in teaching values and moral standards. This TalkSheet offers you that opportunity.

OPENER

How well do your kids know the Ten Commandments? For this intro you'll need a large poster board or whiteboard. Ask your group to think of as many of the Ten Commandments as they can. See if they can remember the order of the Ten Commandments, too. Then take turns reading each command from Exodus 20 with your group. After each one is read, ask your group to put the command in their own words—what does the command mean to them today? Make a master list of all the commandments, written in their own words. Then ask them how and why these commands still apply to people today? Are some more important than others? Why or why not? Which one is the most important and why? How can your kids follow these commands in their own lives? Ask your group to give examples of how society breaks these commandments. Why are some broken more than others?

THE DISCUSSION, BY NUMBERS

1. How did your kids rate society? The world? Take a poll and come to a group consensus on this question. Are the commandments supposed to make people miserable? Why do more and more people live contrary to God's way and discuss the present and future consequences of doing so?

2. You may want to take the time to talk about peer pressure and its influence on individual morality. When do your kids struggle with morality? Why is it hard to decide what's right and wrong?

3. Do your kids agree or disagree? Poll the students on each of the statements and see if they conflict as a group. Take some time to talk about those that they do.

4. What would your high schoolers say to sixth graders? What warnings would they have for them?

5. Each of these passages address Christian morality. Ask several volunteers to complete the sentences, then discuss what they had to say about Christian morality.

THE CLOSE

There's no doubt that the decisions your kids face will get more difficult and uncertain as they grow older. They'll need a moral foundation to base their decision on. People in today's society set their own standards and values—morality is no longer just black or white. Standards that were once clear are now blurred—they've become gray.

Point out that it's hard to stick to a set of values, especially in a society that questions them. Remind them that God has given us a set of morals in the Bible—he's laid out clear boundaries. You may want to read these Ten Commandments (Exodus 20) with your group again, or look back at the set you wrote in the intro. Even though they were written thousands of years ago, how do they still apply today? What other rules does God give in the Bible? What other commands did Jesus give in the New Testament? What benefits come from following God's rules and living for him?

Close by reminding your kids that God forgives and forgets. No one will ever be able to follow God's laws perfectly—that's part of being human. But if someone loves God, they'll follow what he says is best for them. Close with a time of prayer and encourage your kids to start following God's boundaries and asking God for wisdom and guidance in their decisions.

MORE

● You may want to ask your kids to keep track of how many of the Ten Commandments are broken in the next TV show or movie that they watch. Have them note what the movie was rated and what it was about. Follow up with your kids to talk about morals in the media. How common is it for your kids to see murder, adultery, or swearing in what they see? What impact does this have on how people live and treat each other? What can your kids do to set boundaries around themselves?

● Encourage your kids to think of one command that they don't follow very well. What specific area of sin are your kids struggling in? Are they caught up in stealing? Not respecting their parents? Struggle with a low self-esteem (love your neighbor as yourself!). Challenge them to get right with God and to spend some time with him in prayer—he gives strength and wisdom to those who come to him! Encourage them to set goals and see how God works in their lives.

WHO IS THIS GOD ANYWAY?

1. How would you feel in the following situations?
   You've just been told you can never have a close relationship with God.

   You've just been told you can never again attend church.

   You've just been told you are wasting your time on this Christian stuff.

2. On a scale of **1-10 (1 being totally true, 10 being completely untrue)**, how true is this statement for you?
   My relationship with God is the most important relationship I have.

3. Circle the **three words** that best describe God, in your opinion.

Personal	Liberating	Kingly	Feeble
Healing	Mysterious	Blameless	Honest
Eternal	Holy	Accepting	Pure
Strong	Controlling	Merciful	Patient
Angry	Punishing	Passive	Influential
Humorous	Unapproachable	Cruel	Kind
Remote	Sinless	Restrictive	Unaware
Just	Giving	Worthless	Demanding
Loving	True	Protective	Critical
Caring	Friendly	Good	Sovereign
Unchanging	Involved	Forgiving	

4. When do you feel **closest** to God?

5. The prophet Isaiah provides us with a rich description of God. Read the two descriptions in the passages from the Bible—one that describes God and one that describes false gods—then write out what each one says to you.
   Isaiah 44:6-8
   Isaiah 44:9-20

WHO IS THIS GOD ANYWAY? [God]

THIS WEEK

What is God like? Who is he? The Bible says that no one has seen God (John 1:18), yet the Bible is filled with metaphorical descriptions of him. This TalkSheet will help your kids explore their concepts of God and learn to see him through a biblical perspective.

OPENER

Ask for two volunteers to help you introduce this topic. One person should stand away from the group facing the whiteboard or a large piece of newsprint. This person is the artist. The other person, the interpreter, should stand facing the group with their back to the artist. Give the interpreter an object like a light bulb or a coat hanger. The interpreter then explains the object to the artist in such a way that they can accurately draw a picture of it. The interpreter can't look at the artist and the artist can't look at the interpreter. Talk about how this sort of abstract drawing is like our concept of God. We have not seen him ourselves, but we have formed a picture of him through what we have read and heard.

THE DISCUSSION, BY NUMBERS

1. This activity lets kids examine how significant their relationship with God really is. How would they answer each of these questions?

2. The phrase "personal relationship with Jesus Christ" isn't in the Bible. Yet people talk about a personal relationship with Christ in personal metaphors of a friend, a family member, and a spouse. What does it mean to your kids to have a personal relationship with God?

3. How do your kids see God? What words to they use to describe him? You may want to make a master list of these words—then ask why they chose these words. Where did they get these impressions from?

4. People's views of God affect how they view life. If they see God as unapproachable, then they won't take prayer seriously. If they see God as critical, then they'll be hard on themselves. Let volunteers read their completed sentences, then discuss how our thoughts about God affect our actions.

5. Ask the teens to share the different things they learned from the prophet Isaiah about the one true God and false gods.

THE CLOSE

Challenge the group to rethink their view of God. Some people have distorted views of him that limit what God can do in their lives. He commands people not to worship idols, but to focus on him and his power. Pay attention to the views that your kids have. Why have they formed these views of him? What have their parents or teachers taught them about God? Do some of them lack trust in God because of poor relationships with parents? Point out that every person has a unique relationship with God—because everyone relates to him differently!

Close in a time of prayer and encourage your kids to take a few moments with God alone. The best way to understand and get to know God better is to spend some time with him. What are some ways that your kids can get closer to God?

MORE

● Take this discussion further into the Bible. Ask the kids to pick and read five Bible stories. Read the stories with the group and have them write down five new things they learned about God. Explain to them that they can get to know more about God on their own time—doing just the same thing! Getting to know God better means spending time with him!

● Consider doing a more in-depth Bible study with your group or a group of your kids. There are several Bible studies for high schoolers by Youth Specialties, including *Creative Bible Lessons in Psalms*, *Talking the Walk*, and *Downloading the Bible*, including *A Rough Guide to the New Testament* and *A Rough Guide to the Old Testament*. For more information, visit www.YouthSpecialties.com.

HEART TO HEART TALK

1. Rank the following items from **most important (1)** to **least important (10)** in your daily life.

   ❑ Spending time with friends
   ❑ Doing well in school
   ❑ Spending time with God in prayer
   ❑ Looking the best you can
   ❑ Watching TV and surfing the Internet

   ❑ Having a good time
   ❑ Reading the Bible
   ❑ Listening to music
   ❑ Spending time with family
   ❑ Feeling good about who you are

2. What do you think?
   People who pray are generally happier than people who don't pray.

   ❑ Always true
   ❑ Usually true

   ❑ Sometimes true
   ❑ Never true

   Why?

3. Decide which of the following do you think are **A (appropriate)** or **I (inappropriate)** reasons to pray.

   ___ To find a mystical union with God
   ___ To regulate stress in your life
   ___ To take part in spiritual warfare
   ___ To turn inward to find spiritual power
   ___ To spend time in God's presence
   ___ To make yourself feel good.
   ___ To ask God to meet your needs
   ___ To thank God for blessings
   ___ To complain to God about your problems
   ___ To ask God to help others
   ___ To get bailed out of trouble
   ___ To worship and love God
   ___ To request insight to biblical truth
   ___ To do what Christians are supposed to do

4. On the scale below, where would you rank yourself and your prayer habits?

   ◆ |||||||||||||||||||||||||||| ◆

   I pray all the time—I'm the ideal model

   Prayer? What's that again?

5. The following Bible verses are examples of types of prayers. Which verse represents the way you pray?

   Psalm 66:18-20   Matthew 6:9-13   1 Timothy 2:1, 2   1 John 5:14, 15
   Matthew 6:7, 8   Philippians 4:6   James 5:16

From *More High School TalkSheets—Updated!* by David Lynn. Permission to reproduce this page granted only for use in the buyer's own youth group. www.YouthSpecialties.com

HEART TO HEART TALK [prayer]

THIS WEEK

Prayer is an essential part of the Christian life! Your kids need to be encouraged to talk—and to listen—to God. Despite the importance of prayer, many teenagers spend very little time doing it for a number of reasons. Maybe they don't know how to pray, what to ask for, or doubt if God listens. Use this TalkSheet to discuss prayer, its role in Christian growth, and how it brings people closer to God.

OPENER

Ask your kids this question—do they ever notice that when people get stuck in a bind, go through hard times, or feel lost, that's when they call on God for help? That's when the nation and the media talks about God and about prayer. But then the good times come back. And what happens? People go on their way, doing what they want, when they want. But they still expect God to be there for them—at their beckon call.

You may want to bring in a DO NOT DISTURB sign that people hang on their bedroom or hotel room doors. Do your kids ever hang up this sign on their door? Do they ever tell God not to interfere with what's going on in their life? Or do they ever flip the sign over to the maid service side? Why do people always run to God when they want things in their lives cleaned up or fixed? What does God feel about being a convenient God who will be there whenever people want him?

THE DISCUSSION, BY NUMBERS

1. Ask the kids to compare their rankings with the reality of their lives. How far up on the importance ladder should prayer be? If their perception of the importance of prayer in their lives versus the reality of prayer in their lives is inconsistent, explore the reasons why.

2. Does prayer have much to do with happiness and the quality of someone's life? Many Christians who take prayer seriously would say yes! Check out what your kids think.

3. What does prayer mean to your kids? Check out how they responded to these statements. You may want to take a poll of their answers and talk about each one. Why would some reasons for prayer seem more appropriate than others? Which are definitely not good reasons to pray?

4. Where would your kids rank themselves? If you don't want to ask for specific rankings from your group, ask where you think Christian teenagers in general would rank. Would your kids consider prayer to be an important part of their lives? Why or why not?

5. Discuss the different types of prayer examples found in the passages from the Bible. What was different about each one? What models of prayer are the best to follow?

THE CLOSE

Prayer is a conversation between a person and God—just like a chat on the phone with a friend. Encourage your kid to find a prayer style that's comfortable for them and to set a goal for their prayer life—maybe to pray everyday for a short time, to pray a certain time during the day, or whatever works for them. The closer they come to God, the closer he'll come to them (James 4:8).

Close with a time of prayer with your group and them to share their requests and joys with each other. If your group members don't feel comfortable praying out loud, pray out loud for them and give them some time of silent prayer.

MORE

● Your youth group activities calendar can double as a prayer calendar. The next time you create your calendar, write the names of kids and adults involved in your group in each of the daily squares. Point out to your kids that on different days can pray for the specific person listed. Hand out the calendars and encourage your students throughout the month to keep up their prayer support for members of the youth group. Later follow up with them to see how the activity worked and why or why not.

● What's God's model for prayer? Check out the Lord's Prayer with your group. You may want to go through this with your group and break it up into sections. Break your group up into small groups and give each small group a phrase of the Lord's Prayer. Ask them to discuss what the section of prayer means and then write it in their own words. Then together as a group, put all the sections of the prayer together and write a master group interpretation of the Lord's Prayer. Keep this master list for discussion later on and possibly make copies for your kids to take home with them if they need a prayer boost.

GROWING DEEPER

1. How would your life be different if you were **not** a Christian?

2. Which of the following things do you think have helped you grow the most in your faith?
   - ❏ Sharing God with others
   - ❏ Feeling guilty because of sin
   - ❏ Serving others
   - ❏ Praying
   - ❏ Giving money to the church
   - ❏ Going through confirmation
   - ❏ Being part of a small group
   - ❏ Attending church
   - ❏ Walking your talk
   - ❏ Hanging quotes from the Bible in your locker
   - ❏ Reading the Bible
   - ❏ Worshiping God at church
   - ❏ Reading Christian books
   - ❏ Becoming a member of your church
   - ❏ Memorizing Bible verses
   - ❏ Hanging out with Christian friends
   - ❏ Being part of a Bible study
   - ❏ Being baptized
   - ❏ Confessing your sins
   - ❏ Attending youth group
   - ❏ Asking questions
   - ❏ Discussing God with other Christians

3. What do you think? Would you mark each of these **M (me)** or **N (not me)**?
   ___ I have spent time trying to understand my Christian faith.
   ___ I pray in other places besides church.
   ___ I have talked with another Christian about my questions regarding Christianity.
   ___ I try to consider how Jesus might want me to handle my problems.
   ___ I read my Bible in places other than church.
   ___ I have talked with my friends about what it means to be a Christian.
   ___ I am regularly involved in my church's activities.
   ___ I have helped someone in need during the past month.
   ___ I talk over my life decisions with God before I make a choice.
   ___ I believe Christianity is one of the most important influences in my life.
   ___ I have experienced God's love and forgiveness.
   ___ I realize I need God's continual grace and love.
   ___ I attend church more than once a week.

4. Who is **one person** you think most reflects Jesus Christ in their life?

   How do you think you can become more like Jesus?

5. What do the following Bible verses say about **spiritual growth**?
   1 Corinthians 13:12   2 Corinthians 3:18   Hebrews 5:11-14
   1 Corinthians 14:20   Ephesians 3:17-19

From *More High School TalkSheets—Updated!* by David Lynn. Permission to reproduce this page granted only for use in the buyer's own youth group. www.YouthSpecialties.com

GROWING DEEPER [spiritual growth]

THIS WEEK

Christian growth is the process of becoming like Jesus. What a big topic for discussion! Teenagers don't usually discuss this on a day-to-day basis. This TalkSheet discussion can powerfully motivate and encourage Christian growth. Everyone in your group can be a resource to help everyone else grow in Christ.

OPENER

Ask your teens to chart their individual spiritual growth over the past year. The horizontal line should be labeled with the following—one year ago, nine months ago, six months ago, three months ago, and now. Beginning with one year ago, have the kids draw lines representing their spiritual progress. Significant points, high or low, should be indicated by a cross and a comment. For example, a week at camp may be marked with a cross and a comment about its significance. Hanging around with a negative friend may drop the line below the baseline. When they are done, have the kids share their spiritual progress with the group. For example, a student's chart may look like this:

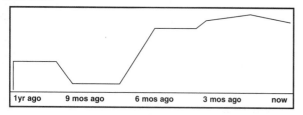

1yr ago   9 mos ago   6 mos ago   3 mos ago   now

THE DISCUSSION, BY NUMBERS

1. Let the kids hypothesize what their lives might be like without Christ. Some kids will think it would be improved, others will see no difference. Allow all the kids to share without being put down. This activity will let you know where your kids are really at. You can then facilitate the discussion more productively.

2. Let your kids share and debate what's been helpful in their Christian life and what hasn't. Have some of these been more effective than others? Why or why not? Why does the church have different activities for different people?

3. Ask kids to resist telling the group what they think the group wants to hear. Encourage honesty and role-model support as the students examine their own lives. Which ones do your kids pick as them? Which ones don't they?

4. A Christian growth role model can be helpful to young and old alike. If people see that others are growing more like Christ, they realize that they can too. Ask volunteers to share why their chosen people are most like Christ. Create a master list of all the ways in which the group can become more like Christ.

5. Ask which passage they would like to discuss first. Focus your attention on that choice. How does it relate to spiritual growth?

THE CLOSE

When people talk about Christian growth, they typically focus on the individual's responsibility to become more like Jesus. But people grow in Christ through community as well as individual focus. That's one reason for the establishment of the church. The context of our growth is the living body of Christ, with him as the head. Take time to close the session by examining with the young people how the church can better promote their Christian growth.

MORE

● It's important for everyone to have spiritual goals. If you feel it's appropriate, ask each of your youth (or those who want to) to write a letter stating their spiritual goals and how they want to grow as Christians. Give them envelopes, which they will address to themselves and seal. Mail the letters to them anywhere from six months to a year.

● Do your kids want to get involved and learn more? You may want to start a small group Bible study and discussion with those who are interested. Check out Youth Specialties (www.YouthSpecialties.com) for some study tools, including the Creative Bible Lessons series and *Downloading the Bible*. You'll also find links to student Web sites (such as www.christianteens.net or www.teens4god.com) where your kids can download devotions, find information, and learn more about how to grow in their faith.

COLORBLIND CHRISTIANITY

1. What do you think about **racism**?
   ❑ There's more racism today than in past years.
   ❑ There's about the same racism today as in past years.
   ❑ There's less racism today than in past years.
   ❑ There's no more racism.

2. What about you? Check the things below that are **true** for you.
   ❑ I've talked with a member of another race about race relations.
   ❑ I would be willing to talk to a member of another race about Jesus Christ.
   ❑ I know someone of another race fairly well.
   ❑ I'd feel comfortable working on a school or church project with a member of another race.
   ❑ I'd want to be close friends with a member of another race.
   ❑ I have a close friend or family member of another race.

3. What do you think? Do you **A (agree)** or **D (disagree)**?
   ___ Teenagers are less racist than adults.
   ___ There's more racism directed toward black people than other minorities.
   ___ Churches have little to offer minorities.
   ___ Minorities should quit blaming their problems on others.
   ___ White people owe other minorities because of past discrimination and injustices.
   ___ Minorities have just as much of an opportunity as others.
   ___ Minorities are as racist as non-minorities.
   ___ It's hard to define what a minority is today.

4. How would you answer these questions—**Y (yes)** or **N (no)**?
   Have you ever—
   ❑ felt you might be prejudice?
   ❑ heard about a racially motivated fight at your school?
   ❑ participated in racial name-calling?
   ❑ been prejudiced against by others?
   ❑ Heard a racial joke that offended you?
   ❑ talked with a member of another race about Jesus Christ?
   ❑ visited a racially hateful Web site?

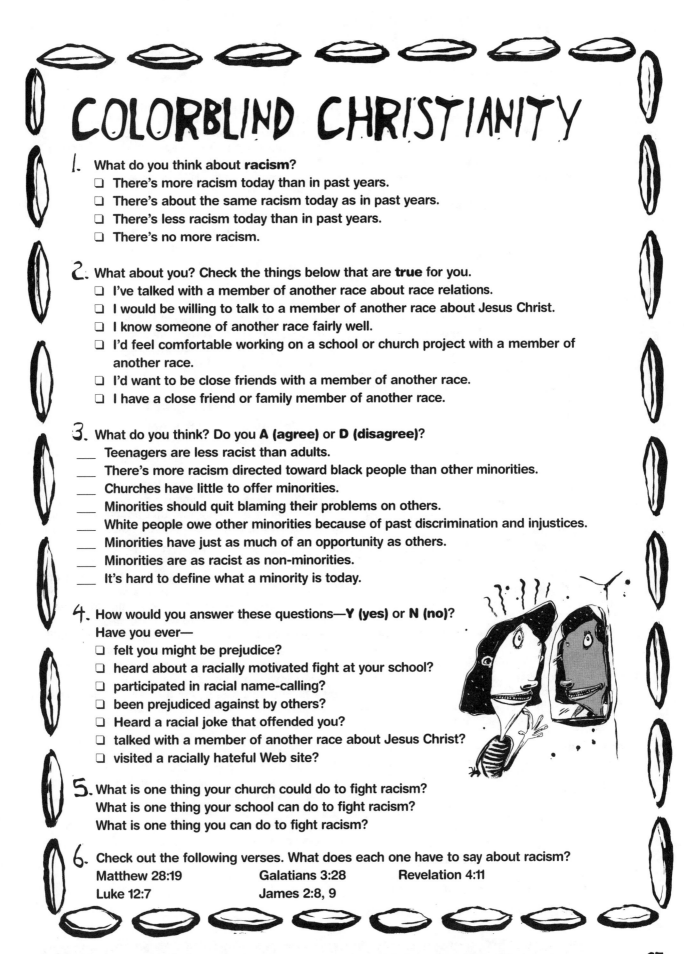

5. What is one thing your church could do to fight racism?
   What is one thing your school can do to fight racism?
   What is one thing you can do to fight racism?

6. Check out the following verses. What does each one have to say about racism?
   Matthew 28:19   Galatians 3:28   Revelation 4:11
   Luke 12:7   James 2:8, 9

From *More High School TalkSheets—Updated!* by David Lynn. Permission to reproduce this page granted only for use in the buyer's own youth group. www.YouthSpecialties.com

COLORBLIND CHRISTIANITY [racism]

THIS WEEK

Despite political correctness and efforts at unity, friction between races is still an issue for some of today's teenagers. Use this TalkSheet to take a look at the state of race relations in your community and your church. Many of people—young and old—verbalize their lack of prejudice and discrimination but still commit acts of bigotry. Racism persists as a problem around the world. Christians, however, can tear down racial lines and respect others—regardless of their color.

OPENER

Break the students into small groups. Ask each group to think of or create a stereotype for a specific group of people—a peer group from school (like the skaters, jocks, surfers, and so on), a race-ethnic group, or an age group like senior citizens. After each group shares the stereotypes, you may want to ask them with these questions—

• What are the assumed ideas about each group?
• How common are these stereotypes among high schoolers and people in general?
• Why do these stereotypes exist?
• Are the stereotypes true? Why or why not?
• Do these ideas help or hurt those being stereotyped?
• Do the stereotypes help you better understand a group of people?

Your kids may have a variety of answers for the opener. Maybe some of them haven't taken a close look at stereotypes before.

As you go through this TalkSheet, be sensitive to members in your group who may be victims of stereotypes and prejudice. Encourage the group to be open-minded and honest, yet sensitive about how they voice their opinions and ideas.

THE DISCUSSION, BY NUMBERS

1. How prevalent do your kids think racism is today? Take a poll of the young people's opinions and group their responses on the scale to get a picture of your group's perception of racism. How do they think this compares with racism in the past?

2. Depending on your community or group, some of your kids may have more contact with minorities than others. For some, this isn't an issue. The more personal and positive contact one has with other races, the less racism exists. Ask your group why some kids may—or may not—feel uncomfortable in close relationships with other races.

3. What do your kids think on these statements? Discuss the statements the teens don't all agree on. If there's one that causes a lot of argument, let them debate the issue.

4. Ask for opinions on each of these statements. These are emotional issues, so don't allow kids to put others down with their responses. Can they back up their responses with support from the Bible? Many of them have most likely not considered what the Bible says about race relations.

5. What can the church do about racism? Are there prejudice attitudes there? What about your kids' schools? What can your kids do to heal or fix damaged race relations?

6. Let the students share their interpretations, then focus on one passage to study. Relate to the group the story of the Good Samaritan (Luke 10:25-37) in which Christ condemns the Jews' hypocrisy as well as their bigotry. The Samaritans were hated by the Jews, yet the Samaritan demonstrated love and mercy in response.

THE CLOSE

The Bible makes it clear that God is opposed to racism—in any form. God clearly says that everyone is equal in his eyes—even the people of Israel that Jews and Gentiles. Because everyone was created equally, they should all be treated equally (Numbers 15:15). Christians should oppose racism and discrimination and live in such a way that people of all races will be drawn to God's redemptive, colorblind love.

MORE

● You may want to ask your group to keep a list of observations about race relations at their schools and in their community for one week. What positive or negative things to they see, hear, or read? How often did it occur? When? What happened and how was it handled? What groups were involved? Was it just racial groups, or was a peer group involved as well?

● Or have your kids surf the Internet for information on hate groups—they are everywhere. Some include skinheads, neo-Nazis, and white supremacists. You may be surprised at what your kids already know about these—they are nearly in every school across the country. Take some time to learn more about these if you don't know anything about these groups. Discuss the motives behind these groups, what issues they are angry about, and what your kids can do to deal with these groups.

BELIEVE IT OR NOT

1. What is **church doctrine**?

2. Do you **agree** or **disagree** with this statement?
   It doesn't matter what doctrine you believe as long as you're a Christian.

3. Put an X by the doctrines below that you think are based on the Bible.

Advent	Baptism	Inspiration	Pantheism	Reconciliation
Agnosticism	Creationism	Islam	Perseverance	Redemption
Amillennialism	Deism	Justification	Pessimism	Sanctification
Anarchy	Hedonism	Mysticism	Petrifaction	The Second
Angelology	Incarnation	Nihilism	Propitiation	The Trinity
Atonement				

4. Go back to question 3 and underline **three doctrines** that you'd like to know more about. Do you know about these or heard about them?

5. How do you think biblical doctrine can make a difference in your life?

6. Check out the following passages of the Bible—what do you think they have in common?
   John 7:16, 17

   Romans 6:17

   Ephesians 4:14

   1 Timothy 1:3-6

   2 John 9, 10

From *More High School TalkSheets—Updated!* by David Lynn. Permission to reproduce this page granted only for use in the buyer's own youth group. www.YouthSpecialties.com

BELIEVE IT OR NOT [biblical doctrine]

THIS WEEK

Since teenagers have so many concerns and problems, youth workers often focus on topical studies of the Bible—like those in this book. Most spend relatively little time on doctrine, even though it is part of the foundation for spiritual maturity and stability. This TalkSheet examines the importance of biblical doctrine and helps your group identify the areas they would like to study.

OPENER

Are your kids familiar with any church doctrine? It's likely that some of your kids won't know the specifics of church doctrine. Others have had classes in church doctrine or catechism. Either way, some doctrines are hard to understand. You may want to explain to your group exactly what a doctrine is. Point out that by reading the Bible and doctrines, they can understand and discern false beliefs and teachings. With the Bible as back up for their faith and what they believe, they will be able to see false religious beliefs differently.

Off the top of their heads, ask your kids to make a list of all the doctrines that they are familiar with. Are they able to name any at all? Throw out a few suggestions to start them out, like redemption, sin, sanctification, or grace. If they seem clueless or lost, that's okay! Start in on the TalkSheet discussion.

THE DISCUSSION, BY NUMBERS

1. Doctrine is the principle or principles of a belief system (it's also known as dogma). Biblical doctrine is a body of principles based on what the Bible teaches about God, salvation, his kingdom, and everything in it.

2. Engage the group in a debate regarding the importance of what people believe and how that affects their Christianity. It's important that our doctrine be based on the Bible because it is unchanging. Interpretations may vary, but God's Word stays the same. Christians should know what the Bible teaches.

3. You may want to have your group list the biblical doctrines. The following are all examples of biblical doctrine—amillennialism, angelology, atonement, baptism, creationism, incarnation, inspiration, justification, perseverance, propitiation, reconciliation, redemption, sanctification, the Second Advent, and the Trinity.

4. Which of these would your kids like to learn more about? Which ones don't they know about? You may want to go ahead and talk about these now or come back to this later.

5. How do beliefs affect the way people live? For example, if you believe in reincarnation, your outlook on life will be different than if you believe in a heaven and a hell.

6. What do these verses have in common? What do these say about church doctrines?

THE CLOSE

Wrap up the discussion by summarizing what was talked about during the TalkSheet. Are your kids more clear on doctrine? Do they still have more questions? Point out to the group that doctrines help Christians discern and protect themselves from false doctrines. By being familiar with doctrine—and having that as a solid foundation for their faith—they'll be able to stand up to deceptive teaching both in the world and in the church.

MORE

- You may want to have your kids do some research on the Internet for information on Christian doctrines—from the list in question 3. Some of these can be pretty heavy subjects—be sure not to overload them! You may want to make this a group effort and work with each other. Or you may want to have your senior pastor or someone else come in to explain these doctrines better.

- Do your kids know what a creed is? Do they have their own personal creed? Using the Apostle's Creed (or another one), have them write a creed—a statement of their personal beliefs. Encourage them to write a creed. put it in a visible place and read it when they start to doubt their beliefs or have people question what they believe and why.

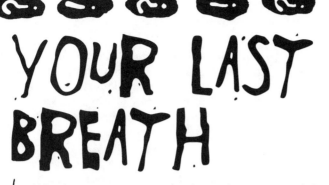

YOUR LAST BREATH

1. Who is one person you've lost who was special to you?

2. Put an arrow by the five most common responses you think teenagers have when a loved one dies.

Shock	Relief	Regret
Denial	Depression	Helplessness
Hurt	Anger	Loneliness
Confusion	Acceptance	Emptiness
Fear	Guilt	
Numbness	Sadness	

3. What do you think—**T (true)** or **F (false)**?
___ Teenagers don't have to worry much about death.
___ Teenagers distance themselves from the elderly because old people are so close to death.
___ Most people aren't prepared to die.
___ People who have a purpose in life have less fear of death.
___ Teenagers have difficulty talking about death.
___ Death is a natural part of the life cycle.
___ God lets some people die for no reason.
___ Young people shouldn't die before older people.
___ Death sometimes freaks me out.
___ The media makes too big a deal about dying.
___ Dying naturally is the same as committing suicide.

4. If you could ask God one question about dying, what would it be?

5. Read the following Bible verses to find out God's perspective on death.
Psalm 16:10   Isaiah 57:1, 2   2 Corinthians 5:6-10
Psalm 49:10-19   1 Corinthians 15:54-57   Hebrews 2:14, 15

From *More High School TalkSheets—Updated!* by David Lynn. Permission to reproduce this page granted only for use in the buyer's own youth group. www.YouthSpecialties.com

YOUR LAST BREATH [death]

THIS WEEK

Death is a topic that more and more must be talked about with kids. An increasing number of young people are preoccupied with death—in their music, through the suicide of a classmate, in their contemplation of the meaning and purpose of life, and especially in the shocking wake of school violence and killings. This TalkSheet faces death in a straightforward manner. By talking about death, you're provided with the opportunity to talk about eternal salvation.

OPENER

This is a sensitive topic—especially for those who have lost someone they've loved. Introduce this topic however you think is best for your group.

You may want to have your kids think about this—if they were to die, what would people say about them? What would they hear their friends saying at their funeral? What does this say about how they live today? Why is it so important to make the most of each day?

You may want to read a story dealing with death or show a movie clip that deals with death. How does the media portray death? How is death talked about in the media? Why do news programs report stories of death, murder, and suicide? Why is the media so caught up in death? How do Christians view death differently than non-Christians?

THE DISCUSSION, BY NUMBERS

1. Many kids will share the experiences they have had with death, such as the death of a grandparent or a pet. Or perhaps they will talk about the suicide of a classmate or the death and destruction themes of some secular music. Be sensitive to young people who are mourning the loss of a friend or family member. Allow kids to share their stories and express their emotions.

2. What are the most common words dealing with death? Take some time to talk about these words. But be particularly sensitive to the issue of suicide.

3. These statements should generate some good healthy debate. Have the kids share their opinions on each one, and give reasons why they feel the way they do.

4. What would your kids ask God about death? You may get a lot of different questions, ranging from cremation to reincarnation and more. Spend some time talking about these questions with your group.

5. What are God's views of death? Take some time to talks about these verses with your group. Do these verses help them understand or deal with death differently? Why or why not? What comfort to they get knowing that there is an afterlife?

THE CLOSE

Use this closing time to point out that the life of each individual involved in this TalkSheet discussion has meaning. It is God who gives life meaning. Because of Christ's work on the cross of Calvary, people can be saved from the despair of a meaningless life and ultimate death.

MORE

● Suicide is a reality in the lives of teenagers—one of the top five causes of death among teenagers and young adults. You may want to spend some time talking about suicide, what causes teen suicide, how to recognize someone who is in danger of taking his or her own life. Visit a few on-line organizations for more information—Suicide Voices Awareness of Education (www.save.org) and the American Foundation for Suicide Prevention (www.afsp.org). If there is a suicide hotline in your area, post the number for the kids to write down. You might also suggest the names of adult counselors in your area who are qualified to provide help to potential suicide victims.

● School violence has also been a cause of teenage death in schools nationwide. You may want to talk about this as well, if you think it's appropriate for your group in your town. Ask your kids what causes teenagers to lash out in violence. Have they seen or experienced situations of school violence? What can your kids do to put an end to school violence and make their own schools safer? For more information, check out the Youth Specialties Web page (www.YouthSpecialties.com) for links and information, including www.disciples.org/violence.htm and Bulletproof? A Student Violence Prevention Program by Neighbors Who Care (www.neighborswhocare.org).

SMUT WORLD

1. Justice Potter Stewart of the U.S. Supreme Court said that he could not define pornography, but that he knows it when he sees it. What would be your definition of **pornography**?

2. What do you think? Do you **A (agree)** or **D (disagree)**?

___ Teenagers who are into pornography won't be affected by it.

___ Limiting the publication, distribution, and sale of sexually explicit material amounts to censorship.

___ TV shows contain material that could be considered pornographic.

___ It's harmless to have pornographic chat room discussions with strangers online.

___ A person can become addicted to pornography.

___ The increase in sex crimes like rape and incest can be partly blamed on the wide spread availability of sexually explicit material.

___ Only child pornography should be outlawed.

___ Most pornography is harmless.

___ Pornography encourages violence toward females.

___ The viewing of sexually explicit material should be legal for people over the age of 21.

___ The more a person is exposed to sexually explicit material, the less likely that person is to develop a healthy sexual outlook.

___ Internet pornography should be banned.

3. Is this statement **true** for you or not?

I wouldn't rent a movie from a store that also rented sexually explicit videos and DVDs.

❏ That's true for me

❏ It depends

❏ That's not true for me

❏ It really doesn't matter to me

4. On the line below, put an X where you think indicates how harmful pornography is to society.

Hardly harmful at all　　　　　　　　　　　　　　　　　　　　　Extremely harmful

5. Study one of the following passages—how does it relate to the issue of pornography?

| 1 Corinthians 6:9-11 | 1 Corinthians 10:31-33 | James 1:13-15 |
| 1 Corinthians 10:11-13 | Ephesians 4:20-24 | 1 John 2:15-17 |

From *More High School TalkSheets—Updated!* by David Lynn. Permission to reproduce this page granted only for use in the buyer's own youth group. www.YouthSpecialties.com

SMUT WORLD [pornography]

THIS WEEK

Pornography is widespread and available to most teenagers who really want it (especially on the Internet!). The tragedy of adolescent involvement is seen daily in the offices of Christian counselors. Their adult clients tell stories of addiction to pornography, of becoming sexually aware as children because of pornography, and of other tragedies directly and indirectly related to their introduction to pornography as children and adolescents. Use this TalkSheet to explore this painful and tragic topic.

OPENER

Write the following ways young people are introduced to pornography on a whiteboard or on newsprint.

Internet porn sites	R-rated movies
National Geographic	NC-17 rated movies
Playboy or *Playgirl*	X-rated movies
Phone sex numbers	Hard-core porn magazines
Soft-core porn magazines	*Sports Illustrated*
Pornographic videos	*Swimsuit Edition*
Victoria's Secret catalog	

Now ask the young people to identify the top three ways students are introduced to pornography. They can add to the list you have created. Point out that these sources are like gateway drugs (caffeine, nicotine, and alcohol that get kids hooked on hardcore drugs) that introduce kids into the world of smut. Tell the group that this TalkSheet focuses on the issue of pornography.

Be sure to review the ground rules found in the introduction of this book—confidentiality is key for this discussion. Many more young people than we realize have been adversely affected by pornography.

THE DISCUSSION, BY NUMBERS

1. You may want to have a dictionary available to look up the word. Ask the group why Justice Potter Stewart's words ring true. Is it because pornography is something you see that arouses sexual desire? Ask the group if there is anything edifying about looking at pornography.

2. Discuss each of these statements, letting the teens express their thoughts on each one. Allow time for disagreements. Once you have completed the discussion, poll the students to determine if they feel that pornography is generally harmful, has mixed effects, or is generally harmless. You can further explore this by asking what harm might come to the average teenager who has only casual exposure to pornography.

3. This is a tough issue that most people who rent movies have never explored. What do your kids think? Should video stores like this be supported? Why or why not?

4. Where did your kids rank the harmfulness of pornography? How has this shown in society? What do your kids think will happen to society of pornography hits kids at younger ages and is more easily accessible via the Internet?

5. Ask the kids which passage they would most like to discuss first. Focus your attention on that choice, asking the group to relate it to the issue of pornography. As time permits, address each of the other five passages.

THE CLOSE

Remind your kids that pornography can seem harmless at first, but can be very dangerous. Help them understand that their initial exposure to pornography may seem innocent, but it can easily grow out of control. Being addicted to porn is like a drug—a serious addiction that ruins lives, alters relationships, and destroys marriages. It ruins a healthy view of sex and distorts the Christian view of love, commitment, and fidelity—it promotes promiscuity and exploits both men and women.

How can your kids deal with pornography in their own lives? How can they shield themselves from being exposed? What can they do if they are hooked already or have friends or family members who are? Encourage them to find help immediately—from a trusted adult, teacher, counselor, or you. And close with prayer with your group, asking for God's wisdom and strength to say no to the temptations all around them.

MORE

● You may want to ask a Christian counselor who is familiar with the addiction process and pornography to speak with your group. She or he can answer questions the young people have as well as discuss some case studies. Let the speaker know that you don't want to include graphic examples—you don't want to be pornographic in discussing pornography, but to talk about the pain and sorrow associated with the victims of pornography.

● For more information on dealing with pornography and helping your kids deal with these issues, check out these Web sites—eXXit (www.exxit.org), Breaking Free from Pornography (www.porn-free.org), Focus on the Family's resources (www.pureintimacy.org), or Caught By the Web (www.caughtbytheweb.com).

GET PLUGGED IN

1. On a scale of 1-10 (**1 being "I'm real involved"** and **10 being "Church? Involved? What?"**) How involved in the church are you?

2. How involved can you see yourself in the church when you're an adult?
   - ❑ I'll regularly attend church services.
   - ❑ I'll make church an important part of my life.
   - ❑ I'll be involved in a number of church activities.
   - ❑ I'll take a leadership role in church.
   - ❑ I think my involvement in church will be a great source of life satisfaction.
   - ❑ I plan to marry someone who sees church involvement as important.
   - ❑ I'll encourage my future family's involvement in church.
   - ❑ I plan to be in a full-time ministry position as a career choice.

3. What do you think of these statements—**T (true)** or **F (false)**?
   ___ Attending church as a child makes living the Christian life easier as a teenager.
   ___ It's normal for teenagers to rebel against the church.
   ___ It's the church's responsibility to motivate a teenager's involvement in church.
   ___ Teenagers should be allowed to attend different churches than their parents.
   ___ Parents and their teenagers need to agree on spiritual matters.
   ___ Most kids would rather go to church by themselves.

4. Place an X on the scale where you see yourself.

   Committed to church   **Rebelling against church**

5. Revelation 2:1-3:22 describes the condition of seven churches. Examine your own life and relationship with God by choosing which condition comes closest to describing your personal spiritual life.
   - ❑ **Church in Ephesus—** Read Revelation 2:1-7
   - ❑ **Church in Smyrna—** Read Revelation 2:8-11
   - ❑ **Church in Pergamum—** Read Revelation 2:12-17
   - ❑ **Church in Thyatira—** Read Revelation 2:18-29
   - ❑ **Church in Sardis—** Read Revelation 3:1-6
   - ❑ **Church in Philadelphia—** Read Revelation 3:7-13
   - ❑ **Church in Laodicea—** Read Revelation 3:14-22

From *More High School TalkSheets—Updated!* by David Lynn. Permission to reproduce this page granted only for use in the buyer's own youth group. www.YouthSpecialties.com

GET PLUGGED IN [church involvement]

THIS WEEK

Church—some young people love it, others do every-thing they can to get out of it! If your kids are like most, they're at different stages of church commit-ment. Use this activity to talk about church involve-ment in a non-threatening manner. Give your kids the chance to express their opinions about the church—both good and bad. You might learn a few things as well!

OPENER

Start by asking your kids an honest question—and ask the group for honest answers. Where would they rather be on a Sunday morning instead of going to church? What would they rather be doing? You'll get a variety of answers. Don't look down on any of your kids! Most of them would probably like to get a few extra hours of sleep. You may want to make a list of these excuses for missing church. Now ask them how they feel when they miss church. They may not feel anything different—some may say they feel guilty or empty afterwards. Talk about what is impor-tant about going to church. Is it more than just showing up and singing some songs? What else goes on a church that's important?

You may want to ask your kids how effective the church services are for them. What makes the church service and being involved in the church good for them? Or not? What do your kids like to be involved in, if anything? Why do they like being involved? What rewards to they get from being a part of a church family? What would they do if they weren't part of a church?

THE DISCUSSION, BY NUMBERS

1. How involved are your kids in their church? What are they involved in? What do they like about being involved in what they do? Why are some kids not involved? Is this a good or bad thing?

2. Provide the kids an opportunity to share their predictions about their own church involvement in one, five, and 10 years down the line. Why would their involvement be different then than now? Why do some churches put more emphasis on adult involvement than on student involvement?

3. Vote on each of these statements, debating any controversial issues that come out of the discus-sion. Some of your kids may have different ideas about some of these statements, depending on their church background and experiences. Spend some time on these if you have time.

4. Where are your kids at on this scale? If you don't want them to share out loud, ask them where the

average teenager their age is. Why are some teenagers on different places on the scale? Why do some see the church as an enemy and rebel?

5. You can also use this activity as a group to examine your church or churches. For every prob-lem that is brought up, ask the group to also sug-gest a solution as well as how they can be a part of that solution.

THE CLOSE

You may want to close this session with a brain-storming activity. Ask your kids to create a list of all the benefits of being involved in church as a teenag-er. Focus on worship, service opportunities, fun times, and personal Christian growth activities. This simple activity can help your young people identify all of the positive opportunities available that they have never considered.

Point out that the church is a body of believers, although it always doesn't feel like one. The church is a giant family—and an important one too. You may want to have some of your kids find verses that talk about the church and what it means to be in a church. There are several references in the New Testament to the church. What verses can they find that describe the church?

Take some time to pray for your church, the church leaders, and the youth of your church. Encourage your kids to pray for how they can get involved in the church as well.

MORE

● You may want to invite some of your church lead-ers to be in on this TalkSheet discussion. This is a convenient opportunity for them to hear what the youth of the church are thinking and feeling. Possibly have a question and answer session after the discussion for the pastor, elders, or committee members to bounce ideas off of your youth and vice versa. Encourage a teamwork approach to the dis-cussion and challenge your kids to continue making suggestions and ideas to the church leaders.

● Consider holding a special service for your kids— or have your kids plan a service for the church. What would they like to see happen in this serv-ice? Would they like a sermon on a specific topic? How singing some of their favorite songs? Encourage them to get involved in the planning. Then debrief on how it was for them to be involved and whether or not they enjoyed the serv-ice more or less.

HOMOPHOBIA

1. Do you know someone who is a **homosexual**—male or female?

2. Name **three fears** that you think heterosexual teenagers might have about homosexuals.

3. What do you think about homosexual activity between two adults who love each other?
   - ❏ God approves of it, and so do I.
   - ❏ God disapproves of it, and so do I.
   - ❏ God approves of it, but I don't.
   - ❏ God disapproves of it, but I don't.

4. What do you think—**Y (yes)**, **N (no)**, or **M (maybe)**?
   ___ Homosexuality is a choice.
   ___ A practicing homosexual couldn't be a Christian.
   ___ Homosexuals can't be changed.
   ___ Homosexuality really isn't that big of a deal.
   ___ The church must reach out to evangelize and disciple more members of the homosexual community.
   ___ Homosexuals aren't much different than you or I.
   ___ Heterosexual sex outside of marriage is just as much a sin as homosexual sex.
   ___ Homosexuals should be willingly accepted into the church.
   ___ There's a difference between being a homosexual and practicing it.

5. If you found out that a friend, family member, or someone you knew was a homosexual, would you think differently of them?

   How would you treat them differently?

6. What would happen in your church if a Christian homosexual were to openly and publicly share their need for Christian love and forgiveness?

7. Read each of the following Bible verses. Which ones apply to homosexual sin? Which ones apply to the homosexual person?
Leviticus 18:22	Romans 1:27, 28	Romans 15:13
Leviticus 20:13	Romans 5:8	1 Corinthians 6:9, 10
Luke 19:9, 10	Romans 8:35	Ephesians 3:16-19

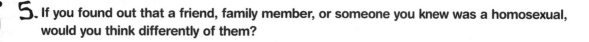

From *More High School TalkSheets—Updated!* by David Lynn. Permission to reproduce this page granted only for use in the buyer's own youth group. www.YouthSpecialties.com

HOMOPHOBIA [homosexuality]

THIS WEEK

Today's young people are growing up in a generation more tolerant of alternative lifestyles. The media tells teenagers that homosexuality is okay, portraying it regularly in movies and TV shows. Use this TalkSheet to discuss with your young people how Christians and the church can love the individual homosexual and hate the sin of homosexuality.

OPENER

Your kids most likely have seen homosexuality portrayed in movies and on TV. To start, ask your kids about gay characters they have seen in movies and on TV. You may want to make a master list of these shows and then ask your kids a few of these questions—

* What are these characters like? How are they portrayed in the movies or on TV?
* Are they primarily guys or girls? Why might one be shown more than the other?
* How the media stereotypes measure up to any gays or lesbians that your kids may know personally?
* How are homosexuals treated in movies and TV as opposed to how they are treated in real life?
* What does society—and the media—in general say about homosexuality?
* How is this the same or different from what the church believes?

Use this discussion as a springboard for talking about Christian values and what the church believes about homosexuality.

THE DISCUSSION, BY NUMBERS

1. Most young people will know of a homosexual acquaintance. If a few do not know any gays or lesbians personally, ask them if they know of any famous homosexuals or homosexual movie or television characters.

2. Create a list of fears and then categorize them into two or three fears. Where do these fears come from? Are these fears legitimate? Are any of these fears influenced the media or society? Or how about the church?

3. The Bible teaches that the homosexual act is a sin, but many young people now see it as an alternative lifestyle no better or worse than other sexual behaviors. As Christians have become more tolerant of sex outside of marriage, they have had to also become more tolerant of homosexual sin. However, sin is sin.

4. Take time to discuss those statements that create disagreement within your group. Which ones, if any, are false assumptions? Which ones are biblically based?

5. How would your kids handle this situation? How have they handled these situations in the past if they've face them? What advice do they have for each other as how to deal with these people? What are the most effective ways to show them Christ's love?

6. Debate this question to see how open your church handles homosexuality? Is it willing to reach out in the name of Jesus? What would your kids to differently? How do they expect the church to change in the coming years on this issue?

7. Leviticus 18:22, Leviticus 20:13, Romans 1:27, 28, and 1 Corinthians 6:9, 10 all focus on the sin of homosexuality. The other passages all deal with God's love for the sinner. Ask the group to determine why it is so difficult for most Christians to separate the sin from the sinner when it comes to homosexuality.

THE CLOSE

Some teenagers in your group may be experimenting with homosexual behaviors. They need God's forgiveness and grace just like teenagers who experiment with heterosexual behavior.

Some teenagers and adults persist in their homosexuality, claiming that it's genetically based or that they grew up in a dysfunctional, abusive family. Whatever the cause, homosexuals need to hear that Christ died for them. They don't need name-calling, discriminatory actions, or homophobia. The Bible clearly teaches that homosexuality is a sin—a shameful and unnatural act—but Christ came to forgive sin and to love sinners. We can do no less.

MORE

● You may want to ask a group of parents to attend the session and talk about their views on the subject. Be sure to choose the parents carefully. It's important that they are respectful of homosexuals and the opinions of your kids. Encourage your group members to ask questions and debate the issue among themselves.

● If you need or would like more information to Christian links on this topic, check out Hope for Teens (www.hopeforteens.com), Exodus International North America (www.exodus-northamerica.org), National Association for Research and Therapy of Homosexuality (www.narth.com), Loving Grace Ministry, Inc. (www.lovinggraceministry.org), or Eagles' Wings Ministry (www.ewm.org).

GOT FAITH?

1. If you took a test that showed how seriously you lived out your faith in Jesus Christ, what grade do you think you'd receive (A, B, C, D, F)?

2. If your friends at school graded the test, what grade would they give you?

3. What do you think?
   Faith is believing in something—
   ❑ that you know isn't true.
   ❑ that you can't prove.
   ❑ that you can't see.
   ❑ that you trust in.

4. Why don't some Christians your age take their faith seriously? Choose **three reasons** from the list below.
   ❑ Christianity isn't fun.
   ❑ Christianity may not be true.
   ❑ Christianity doesn't work in everyday life.
   ❑ Christianity is too hard.
   ❑ Christianity is irrelevant to everyday life.
   ❑ Christianity doesn't make you popular.
   ❑ Christianity gets lost in busy lives.
   ❑ Christianity doesn't make much sense.
   ❑ Christianity is boring.
   ❑ Christianity is too confusing.
   ❑ Christianity is for old people who are about to die.
   ❑ Other—

5. How do you think your faith will change as you get older?

6. Check out Hebrews 11—what **three things** does it say about faith?

From *More High School TalkSheets—Updated!* by David Lynn. Permission to reproduce this page granted only for use in the buyer's own youth group. www.YouthSpecialties.com

GOT FAITH? [faith]

THIS WEEK

Even if they aren't aware of it, everyone has faith. Some have faith in themselves, some in science, and some in money. Others put their faith in cults or false religions. Take time to talk about what kind of faith your students have through a TalkSheet discussion.

OPENER

What is the importance of faith? What does faith mean to your kids? Start out by asking your kids a few questions to get them rolling. Why do people—both non-Christians and Christians—have faith in something? What purpose or direction does faith give people? Point out to your kids that people find hope in what they have faith in. For some people, faith is empty and numb. It doesn't mean anything to them. What faiths have your kids noticed in others at school? In their families? On the job? What do people today put their faith in and why? You may want to make a master list of these suggestions. What does it mean to have faith in a person? How does this relate to having faith in God?

THE DISCUSSION, BY NUMBERS

1. Did the grades they chose reflect how seriously they live out their faith? Why or why not? You may want to ask a few of them to share their grades and why they gave themselves that grade.

2. Have students compare the grades they gave themselves with the grades they feel their friends might give them. Is there a difference between the two grades? Why or why not?

3. What do your kids think about this statement? What are your students are putting their faith into—the church, a set of beliefs found in a book, a quest for the meaning of life, or a historical Jesus who is who he says he is?

4. Examine the reasons your kids believe some young people don't take their faith seriously. What distracts teenagers from their faith? Also examine why some young people do take their faith seriously. Is it easier for young people to live with or without faith in Christ? Is the Christian life worth it?

5. Explore how someone's faith may change throughout life, especially during the next stage of life—the college-career years. Talk about whether or not the students' faith will be strengthened or weakened by questioning their beliefs and faith. Will it become more or less important?

6. Create a master list of everyone's responses. Take one or two of the Bible characters mentioned in Hebrews 11 and review their relationships to faith.

THE CLOSE

Explain that many people talk about faith in terms of belief. They believe that there is a God or they believe that you should go to church. But is simple believing that faith the kind of faith God wants? There isn't anything wrong with a belief that focuses on information. The Bible says that even the demons believe (James 2:19). But there is another kind of faith—a faith that believes in something. It is based on facts, but runs deeper than mere knowledge. It focuses on a relationship with God. Your kids should understand that God didn't expect them to walk around lost and in the dark—the Bible provides them with the facts for their faith. But they still must believe in those facts to have a personal relationship with Jesus Christ.

MORE

● Hold a faith Q&A time with your group. Have the group write down any questions they have about the Christian faith on 3x5 cards (anonymously). Then collect the cards and have your kids take turns picking out questions. If they feel comfortable, have them try to answer it or pass it on. Discuss the questions as a group and encourage them to use the Bible for back up to their questions and answers. To liven things up, invite your senior pastor to a meeting and put him in the hot seat for a question-and-answer session!

● Challenge your kids to e-mail or talk with one adult this week about their belief in God, life after death, the Bible, miracles, prayer, and so on. Or, challenge them to go into an on-line chat room to get some responses on these questions. This is a great way to challenge others to think about and defend their beliefs. Especially if they enter chatrooms under non-Christian Web pages! Later have them share their experiences, what was discussed and what the kids learned from doing this.

RESOURCES FROM YOUTH SPECIALTIES

YOUTH MINISTRY PROGRAMMING

Camps, Retreats, Missions, & Service Ideas (Ideas Library)
Compassionate Kids: Practical Ways to Involve Your Students in Mission and Service
Creative Bible Lessons from the Old Testament
Creative Bible Lessons in 1 & 2 Corinthians
Creative Bible Lessons in John: Encounters with Jesus
Creative Bible Lessons in Romans: Faith on Fire!
Creative Bible Lessons on the Life of Christ
Creative Bible Lessons in Psalms
Creative Junior High Programs from A to Z, Vol. 1 (A-M)
Creative Junior High Programs from A to Z, Vol. 2 (N-Z)
Creative Meetings, Bible Lessons, & Worship Ideas (Ideas Library)
Crowd Breakers & Mixers (Ideas Library)
Downloading the Bible Leader's Guide
Drama, Skits, & Sketches (Ideas Library)
Drama, Skits, & Sketches 2 (Ideas Library)
Dramatic Pauses
Everyday Object Lessons
Games (Ideas Library)
Games 2 (Ideas Library)
Games 3 (Ideas Library)
Good Sex: A Whole-Person Approach to Teenage Sexuality and God
Great Fundraising Ideas for Youth Groups
More Great Fundraising Ideas for Youth Groups
Great Retreats for Youth Groups
Holiday Ideas (Ideas Library)
Hot Illustrations for Youth Talks
More Hot Illustrations for Youth Talks
Still More Hot Illustrations for Youth Talks
Ideas Library on CD-ROM
Incredible Questionnaires for Youth Ministry
Junior High Game Nights
More Junior High Game Nights
Kickstarters: 101 Ingenious Intros to Just about Any Bible Lesson
Live the Life! Student Evangelism Training Kit
Memory Makers
The Next Level Leader's Guide
Play It! Over 150 Great Games for Youth Groups
Roaring Lambs
Special Events (Ideas Library)
Spontaneous Melodramas
Spontaneous Melodramas 2
Student Leadership Training Manual
Student Underground: An Event Curriculum on the Persecuted Church
Super Sketches for Youth Ministry
Talking the Walk
Teaching the Bible Creatively
Videos That Teach
What Would Jesus Do? Youth Leader's Kit
Wild Truth Bible Lessons
Wild Truth Bible Lessons 2
Wild Truth Bible Lessons—Pictures of God
Wild Truth Bible Lessons—Pictures of God 2
Worship Services for Youth Groups

PROFESSIONAL RESOURCES

Administration, Publicity, & Fundraising (Ideas Library)
Dynamic Communicators Workshop
Equipped to Serve: Volunteer Youth Worker Training Course
Help! I'm a Junior High Youth Worker!
Help! I'm a Small-Group Leader!
Help! I'm a Sunday School Teacher!
Help! I'm a Volunteer Youth Worker!
How to Expand Your Youth Ministry
How to Speak to Youth...and Keep Them Awake at the Same Time
Junior High Ministry (Updated & Expanded)
The Ministry of Nurture: A Youth Worker's Guide to Discipling Teenagers
Postmodern Youth Ministry
Purpose-Driven® Youth Ministry
Purpose-Driven® Youth Ministry Training Kit
***So That's* Why I Keep Doing This! 52 Devotional Stories for Youth Workers**
A Youth Ministry Crash Course
Youth Ministry Management Tools
The Youth Worker's Handbook to Family Ministry

ACADEMIC RESOURCES

Four Views of Youth Ministry & the Church
Starting Right: Thinking Theologically About Youth Ministry

DISCUSSION STARTERS

Discussion & Lesson Starters (Ideas Library)
Discussion & Lesson Starters 2 (Ideas Library)
EdgeTV
Get 'Em Talking
Keep 'Em Talking!
Good Sex: A Whole-Person Approach to Teenage Sexuality & God
High School TalkSheets—Updated!
More High School TalkSheets—Updated!
High School TalkSheets Psalms and Proverbs—Updated!
Junior High and Middle School TalkSheets—Updated!
More Junior High and Middle School TalkSheets—Updated!
Junior High and Middle School TalkSheets Psalms and Proverbs—Updated!
Real Kids: Short Cuts
Real Kids: The Real Deal—on Friendship, Loneliness, Racism, & Suicide
Real Kids: The Real Deal—on Sexual Choices, Family Matters, & Loss
Real Kids: The Real Deal—on Stressing Out, Addictive Behavior, Great Comebacks, & Violence
Real Kids: Word on the Street
Unfinished Sentences: 450 Tantalizing Statement-Starters to Get Teenagers Talking & Thinking
What If...? 450 Thought-Provoking Questions to Get Teenagers Talking, Laughing, and Thinking
Would You Rather...? 465 Provocative Questions to Get Teenagers Talking
Have You Ever...? 450 Intriguing Questions Guaranteed to Get Teenagers Talking

ART SOURCE CLIP ART

Stark Raving Clip Art (print)
Youth Group Activities (print)
Clip Art Library Version 2.0 CD-ROM

DIGITAL RESOURCES

Clip Art Library Version 2.0 CD-RPOM
Ideas Library on CD-ROM
Youth Ministry Management Tools

VIDEOS AND VIDEO CURRICULUMS

Dynamic Communicators Workshop
EdgeTV
Equipped to Serve: Volunteer Youth Worker Training Course
The Heart of Youth Ministry: A Morning with Mike Yaconelli
Live the Life! Student Evangelism Training Kit
Purpose-Driven® Youth Ministry Training Kit
Real Kids: Short Cuts
Real Kids: The Real Deal—on Friendship, Loneliness, Racism, & Suicide
Real Kids: The Real Deal—on Sexual Choices, Family Matters, & Loss
Real Kids: The Real Deal—on Stressing Out, Addictive Behavior, Great Comebacks, & Violence
Real Kids: Word on the Street
Student Underground: An Event Curriculum on the Persecuted Church
Understanding Your Teenager Video Curriculum
Youth Ministry Outside the Lines: The Dangerous Wonder of Working with Teenagers

STUDENT RESOURCES

Downloading the Bible: A Rough Guide to the New Testament
Downloading the Bible: A Rough Guide to the Old Testament
Grow For It Journal through the Scriptures
So What Am I Gonna Do With My Life? Journaling Workbook for Students
Spiritual Challenge Journal: The Next Level
Teen Devotional Bible
What (Almost) Nobody Will Tell You about Sex
What Would Jesus Do? Spiritual Challenge Journal
Wild Truth Journal for Junior Highers
Wild Truth Journal—Pictures of God
Wild Truth Journal—Pictures of God 2

SO YOU WANNA GET YOUR KIDS TALKING ABOUT REAL-LIFE ISSUES?

Then don't miss the full set of updated TalkSheets!

JUNIOR HIGH • MIDDLE SCHOOL TALKSHEETS—UPDATED!

MORE JUNIOR HIGH • MIDDLE SCHOOL TALKSHEETS—UPDATED!

JUNIOR HIGH • MIDDLE SCHOOL TALKSHEETS PSALMS & PROVERBS—UPDATED!

HIGH SCHOOL TALKSHEETS—UPDATED!

MORE HIGH SCHOOL TALKSHEETS—UPDATED!

HIGH SCHOOL TALKSHEETS PSALMS & PROVERBS—UPDATED!

www.YouthSpecialties.com